Integrated Chinese

LEVEL 1

Part 2

Integrated Chinese

中文听说读写

Traditional & Simplified Character Edition

CHARACTER WORKBOOK

2nd Edition

Tao-chung Yao and Yuehua Liu

Jeffrey J. Hayden, Xiaojun Wang, Yea-fen Chen,

Liangyan Ge, Nyan-Ping Bi & Yaohua Shi

CHENG & TSUI COMPANY ▲ Boston

Second Edition

12 11 10 09 08 5 6 7 8

Published by
Cheng & Tsui Company, Inc.
25 West Street
Boston, MA 02111-1213 USA
Fax (617) 426-3669
www.cheng-tsui.com
"Bringing Asia to the World"™

Integrated Chinese Level 1 Part 2 Character Workbook
Traditional & Simplified Character Edition
ISBN 978-0-88727-439-8

The *Integrated Chinese* series includes textbooks, workbooks, character workbooks, audio products, multimedia products, teacher's resources, and more. Visit **www.cheng-tsui.com** for more information on the other components of *Integrated Chinese*.

Printed in Canada

THE INTEGRATED CHINESE SERIES

The *Integrated Chinese* series is a two-year course that includes textbooks, workbooks, character workbooks, audio CDs, CD-ROMs, DVDs, and teacher's resources.

Textbooks introduce Chinese language and culture through a series of dialogues and narratives, with culture notes, language use and grammar explanations, and exercises.

Workbooks follow the format of the textbooks and contain a wide range of integrated activities that teach the four language skills of listening, speaking, reading, and writing.

Character Workbooks help students learn Chinese characters in their correct stroke order. Special emphasis is placed on the radicals that are frequently used to compose Chinese characters.

Audio CDs include the narratives, dialogues and vocabulary presented in the textbooks, as well as pronunciation and listening exercises that correspond to the workbooks.

Teacher's Resources contain answer keys, transcripts of listening exercises, grammar notes, and helpful guidance on using the series in the classroom.

Multimedia CD-ROMs are divided into sections of listening, speaking, reading, and writing, and feature a variety of supplemental interactive games and activities for students to test their skills and get instant feedback.

In the **Workbook DVD,** the dialogues from the Level 1 Part 1 Workbook are presented in contemporary settings in color video format.

PUBLISHER'S NOTE

When *Integrated Chinese* was first published in 1997, it set a new standard with its focus on the development and integration of the four language skills (listening, speaking, reading, and writing). Today, to further enrich the learning experience of the many users of *Integrated Chinese* worldwide, the Cheng & Tsui Company is pleased to offer the revised, updated and expanded second edition of *Integrated Chinese*. We would like to thank the many teachers and students who, by offering their valuable insights and suggestions, have helped *Integrated Chinese* evolve and keep pace with the many positive changes in the field of Chinese language instruction. *Integrated Chinese* continues to offer comprehensive language instruction, with many new features.

The Cheng & Tsui Asian Language Series is designed to publish and widely distribute quality language learning materials created by leading instructors from around the world. We welcome readers' comments and suggestions concerning the publications in this series. Please send feedback to our Editorial Board members in care of **editor@cheng-tsui.com**.

CONTENTS

Preface xi

Lessons

Lesson 12: Dining 吃飯. 1
Lesson 13: At the Library 在圖書館 13
Lesson 14: Asking Directions 問路 23
Lesson 15: Birthday Party 生日晚會. 33
Lesson 16: Seeing a Doctor 看病 43
Lesson 17: Dating 約會 53
Lesson 18: Renting an Apartment 租房子. 61
Lesson 19: Post Office 郵局 71
Lesson 20: On Sports 運動 79
Lesson 21: Travel 旅行 91
Lesson 22: Hometown 家鄉. 101
Lesson 23: At the Airport 在機場 113

Indexes

Enlarged Characters for Easier Viewing 125
Character Index (Chronological by Lesson). 129
Character Index (Alphabetical by Pīnyīn) 135
Character Index: Traditional (Arranged by Stroke Count) 147
Character Index: Simplified (Arranged by Stroke Count) 159
Glossary: English-Chinese. 169
Character Index: Traditional (Arranged by Radical). 183
Character Index: Simplified (Arranged by Radical) 193

PREFACE

This Character Workbook is a companion volume to *Integrated Chinese* Textbook, Level 1, Part 2. The *Integrated Chinese* series is an acclaimed, best-selling introductory course in Mandarin Chinese. With its holistic, integrated focus on the four language skills of listening, speaking, reading, and writing, it teaches all the basics beginning and intermediate students need to function in Chinese. *Integrated Chinese* helps students understand how the Chinese language works grammatically, and how to use Chinese in real life.

This book is designed to help students learn Chinese characters in their correct stroke order, and then by their components. We believe that the student will learn a new character more easily if s/he can identify the components in each character and know why the specific components are used in each character. Therefore we strongly urge teachers to teach their students the 40 basic radicals (introduced at the beginning of the Level 1, Part 1 Character Workbook), which are frequently used to compose Chinese characters.

The Importance of Learning Radicals

When learning a new character, the first thing that the student should do is to try to identify the known component(s). By doing that, the student will only need to remember what components are in the character, rather than remember the composition of many meaningless strokes. For example, both 女 (nǚ, *female*) and 馬 (mǎ, *horse*) are taught in the radical section. When the student sees the character 媽 (mā, *mother*) in Lesson 2, s/he should be able to tell that the new character 媽 consists of two known components, namely, 女 and 馬. The components in a character sometimes give clues to the meaning and pronunciation of the character. The radical 女 in the character 媽 suggests that the character might be related to females, and the other component, 馬, is a phonetic element giving a clue to its pronunciation. If a student can remember that the character for "mother" sounds like "horse," he/she would have an easier time learning how to write the character. It would be a very painful way to learn the character 媽 if all one sees is a character consisting of a number of meaningless strokes, with a few vertical lines, a few horizontal lines, and a few dots.

How This Book Is Designed

Each page of this Character Workbook has four to five new characters on it. Each new character is displayed in a large point size on the left side of the page, with the traditional (complex) form on the left and the simplified form on the right. The *pīnyīn* reading and English translation are immediately to the right of these. An asterisk (*) before an English translation means that the character is bound to another character and that the English translation represents the meaning of the compound rather than the individual character. Next to the *pīnyīn* reading there is a number in parentheses, which represents the ranking of the character given in the *Xiàndài Hànyǔ Pínlǜ Cídiǎn* (《现代汉语频率词典》, *The Dictionary of Modern Chinese Word Frequency*). For example, for the character 人 (rén, *person*), the number "9" given in the parentheses means that this character is the ninth most frequently used character in the Chinese written language. The symbol "†" in the parentheses indicates that the character does not belong to the 1000 most frequently used characters according to the *Xiàndài Hànyǔ Pínlǜ Cídiǎn.* While we try to introduce the first 1000 most frequently used characters in the first two levels of *Integrated Chinese*, we sometimes have to include some characters beyond the first thousand to make the text natural and functional.

In the "Radicals" section, under the English translation of the character, the same radical is found in a smaller size. If the radical has a variation, then the variation is given to the right of the smaller character. If the radical has a simplified version, this is given in the third square. Of the 40 most common radicals introduced (see the Level 1, Part 1 Character Workbook), there are only three radicals that have stand-alone simplified characters: 貝 (贝), 門 (门), and 馬 (马). The other simplifications (abbreviations) must be used as components within characters.

In the main lessons, both traditional and simplified characters are provided together. Both forms will have the strokes numbered. Immediately to the right of the large character(s), underneath the *pīnyīn* and English definition, are smaller versions of the character(s). The first will show the radical of the character in black, with the rest of the character in gray. When a simplified version of the character exists, it is given to the right of the smaller traditional character. If a variant of the character exists, it will be provided in the third square and will have the small symbol "Δ" after it indicating the "printing/variant form." Students should learn how to write the "written form," i.e., the large character.

Each practicing unit for a character contains three or four rows of small boxes. The first row to the right of the *pīnyīn* and English has two grayed characters. The student is expected to trace these. If the character has a simplified form, this will appear underneath the grayed traditional characters. The final three boxes at the end of the first and second rows are in graph-style layout to facilitate practice of character proportion. The remaining row(s) have at their head (the far left) small versions of the character (traditional, and, where one exists, simplified). To the right of these the characters have been penned in according to their proper stroke orders. The remaining empty boxes are for the student to practice writing the character in free form. By this time in the process, the student should be expected to be able to draw the character in proper spatial proportions without the use of any guides.

It is very important that each character is drawn in the correct stroke order. Two devices are used in this workbook to show a character's stroke order. The small numbers printed along the large characters indicate the sequence of the strokes. In general, every effort has been made to place the number at the starting point of the stroke. Because in some instances it is not very easy to tell which number goes with what stroke, or to tell where each stroke begins and ends, a "pen version" of each character is provided. Immediately below the large character, the character is drawn one step at a time to show how it is formed. Students should consult this series of strokes when practicing writing characters.

For components that have previously appeared, the pen version may simply show the entire component already drawn rather than writing it out one stroke at a time. For example, the pen version for the character 胖 (pàng, *fat*) in Lesson 20 uses only two boxes, one for 月, and one for 半. This means that when writing the character 胖, one first writes 月, and then one writes 半 next to 月 to form 胖. No individual strokes are given here because the student has already learned how to write 月 and 半 separately (see Lesson 3).

Additional Resources

There are many computer programs (such as *Chinese Character Tutor* by Ted Yao and Mark Peterson and *Hanzi Assistant* by Panda Software) that are designed to teach stroke order. Students are encouraged to use them if they have access to the software. For more information on computer software for learning Chinese characters, and to share ideas with other users of the *Integrated Chinese* series, please visit http://EALL.hawaii.edu/yao/ICUsers/. Jeffrey J. Hayden has also created printable flash cards covering all the characters introduced in this textbook. These and many other materials related to *Integrated Chinese* may be found at http://www2.hawaii.edu/~jeffrey/.

To learn more about the *Integrated Chinese* series, get the latest product updates, and find other supplementary resources, please visit the official *Integrated Chinese* website by going to **http://www.cheng-tsui.com/contact.asp**, and clicking on the link for the *Integrated Chinese* website.

About This New Edition

The three people who have spent the most time in preparing this version of the *Integrated Chinese* Level 1 Part 2 Character Workbook are Jeffrey J. Hayden, Xiaojun Wang, and Ted Tao-chung Yao. Based on suggestions provided by teachers at the Chinese Language Instructional Materials (CLIM) conference held in Honolulu in July 2003, Hayden incorporated his design model for the *Integrated Chinese* Level 2 Character Workbook into this combined traditional/simplified edition, which includes material previously designed for the separate traditional and simplified editions of the *Integrated Chinese* Level 1 Character Workbooks. Wang has again done the pen version stroke ordering in this edition.

Dialogue I

務	务	wù (376) *service

務	予	矛	敄	務
务	ノ	夂	务	

桌	zhuō (869) table

桌	ｌ	⺊	占	桌

菜	菜	cài (707) vegetable; dish

菜	艹	廾	艹	艹	艹	菜
菜	艹	廾	艹	艹	艹	菜

餃	饺	jiǎo (†) dumpling

餃	食	餃
饺	饣	饺

菜 菜 菜

素		sù (766) white; plain			素	素				
		素								
素	龶	素								

盤	盘	pán (850) plate; dish			盤	盤				
		盤	盘		盘	盘				
盤	㇒	丿	力	月	舟	舟	般	盤		
盘	㇒	丿	力	舟	舟	舟	盘			

豆		dòu (†) bean			豆	豆				
		豆								
豆	一	口	戸	豆	豆					

腐		fǔ (†) rotten; stale			腐	腐				
		腐								
腐	广	广	府	府	腐	腐	腐			

肉		ròu (866) meat			肉	肉				
		肉	肉							
肉	肉									

碗
wǎn (996)
bowl
碗 一 丆 石 石宀 石夕 石夗 碗

酸
suān (†)
sour
酸 酉 酉厶 酉夊 酸

辣
là (†)
hot; spicy
辣 立 辛 辣

湯 汤
tāng (†)
soup
湯 氵 湯
汤 氵 汤

放
fàng (163)
to put in; to add
放 方 放

Character	Pinyin	No.	Meaning	Components / stroke sequence
味	wèi	(822)	flavor	味 口 味
精	jīng	(459)	essence	精 米 精
渴	kě	(†)	thirsty	渴 氵 … 渴
些	xiē	(92)	some	些 止 此 些
夠 够	gòu	(380)	enough	夠 多 … 夠; 够 勹 句 够

餓	饿	è (饣)		餓	餓
		to be hungry		饿	饿
		餓	饿		
餓	食	餓			
饿	饣	饿			

餓 餓 餓

Dialogue II

傅		fù (†) teacher	傅	傅			
		傅					
傅	亻	仁	亻	俌	俌	俌	傅

糖		táng (†) sugar	糖	糖			
		糖					
糖	米	籵	粐	粐	糖		

醋		cù (†) vinegar	醋	醋			
		醋					
醋	酉	醋					

魚	鱼	yú (537) fish	魚	鱼	魚	鱼	
					鱼	鱼	
魚	ク	鱼	魚				
鱼	ク	鱼	鱼				

甜		tián (†) sweet	甜	甜			
		甜	甜				
甜	舌	舌	甜	甜	甜	甜	

極	极	jí	(389)
		extreme	
燒	烧	shāo	(684)
		to burn, cook	
牛		niú	(779)
		cow; ox	
賣	卖	mài	(591)
		to sell	

賣 賣 賣

完 wán (251) to finish

完 宀 宀 宁 完

拌 bàn (†) mix

拌 扌 拌

瓜 guā (†) melon

瓜 ㇒ 𠂆 𠂊 𤓰 瓜

米 mǐ (430) rice

米 米

Fun With Characters

I. Crossword Puzzle.

Fill in the squares by providing translations for the cues given below.

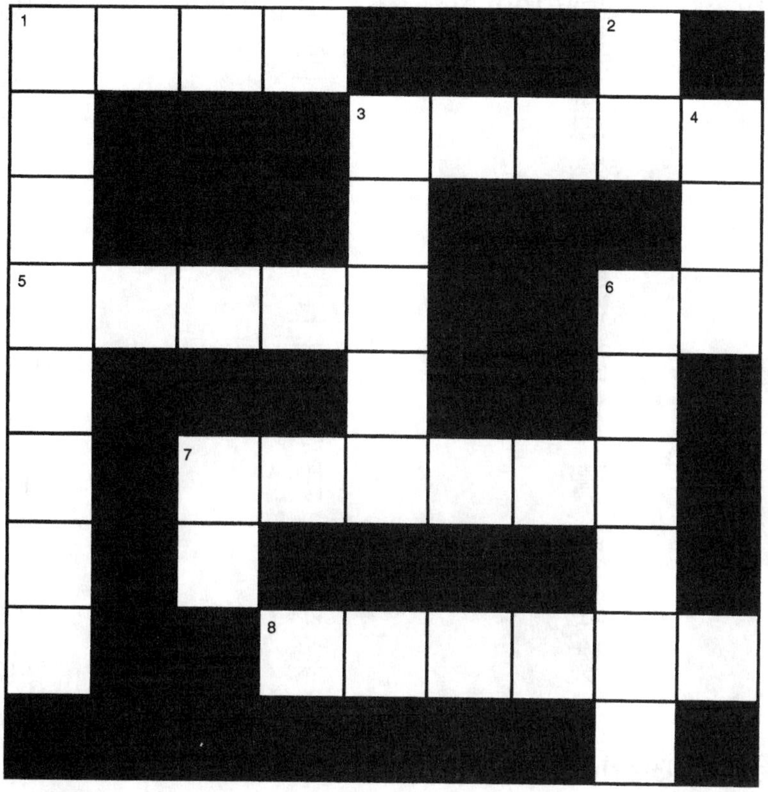

Across

1. Good morning, Teacher Wang
3. Wang Peng also eats (a meal)
5. Li You is a student
6. there
7. Please serve the dishes quickly.
8. Why are there so many people?!

Down

1. Wang Peng and Li You are both vegetarians.
2. delicious
3. Mr. Wang orders dishes.
4. restaurant
6. Then, what will (you) be drinking (then)?
7. to treat (someone)

II. Radical Identification.

Provide the Pīnyīn for each of the following characters and put the radical component each set has in common in the parentheses to the right.

糖 ______ 精 ______ 糟 ______ (____)

渴 ______ 汽 ______ 湯 (汤) ______ (____)

桌 ______ 菜 (菜) ______ 極 (极) ______ (____)

燒 (烧) ______ 煩 (烦) ______ 熱 (热) ______ (____)

III. Matching.

First, draw a line connecting the Pīnyīn to its traditional character. Then, connect the traditional character to its simplified counterpart. Finally, draw a line connecting the simplified character to its English meaning.

Pīnyīn	Traditional	Simplified	English
cài	務	鱼	enough
è	魚	务	extreme
gòu	夠	汤	to be hungry
jí	菜	烧	to burn
jiǎo	湯	盘	to sell
mài	盤	卖	dumpling
pán	極	饺	fish
shāo	賣	极	plate
tāng	餃	够	service
wù	餓	饿	soup
yú	燒	菜	vegetable

IV. Phonological Distinction.

Provide the **full** Pīnyīn for each of the following characters and then put the basic homonym (initial + final, but no tone) each set shares in the parentheses to the right.

可	______	渴	______	客	______	(_____)
位	______	喂	______	味	______	(_____)
天	______	田	______	甜	______	(_____)
完	______	碗	______	灣 (湾)	______	(_____)
五	______	午	______	務 (务)	______	(_____)
半	______	拌	______	辦 (办)	______	(_____)
京	______	精	______	經 (经)	______	(_____)
機 (机)	______	極 (极)	______	幾 (几)	______	(_____)

Dialogue I

| 借 | | | jiè (†)
to borrow | | 借 | 借 | | | | |
| 借 | 亻 | 借 | | | | | | | | |

帶	带	dài (261) belt; tape		带	带				
		帶	带	带	带				
帶	一	卅	卅	卅	卅	带			
带	一	十	卅	卅	卅	带			

職	职	zhí (†) duty; job		職	职				
		職	职	職	职				
see page 123									
職	耳	晬	職	職	職				
职	耳	耴	职						

把			bǎ (57) Preposition		把	把			
		把							
把	扌	把							

職　　　職　　　職

證 证

zhèng *(584)*

evidence; certificate

證 证

證 言 證 證

证 讠 讠 订 证 证 证

留

liú *(616)*

leave (behind); remain

留

留 留

言

yán *(655)*

word

言

言 言

實 实

shí *(109)*

reality

實 实

實 宀 實 實

实 宀 宀 实

證 證 證

驗	验	yàn (443) to examine; to check

see page 123

驗 馬 … 驗

验 马 … 验

樓	楼	lóu (†) floor; storey

樓 木 … 樓

楼 木 … 楼

忘	wàng (810) to forget

忘 亡 忘

其	qí (253) he; she; it; they

其 一 十 廾 甘 甘 其 其

卡 — kǎ (†) — to block; to check

卡 ⺊ 卞 卡

關 关 — guān (203) — to close

關 門 門 閞 閞 關 關 關 關

关 丷 关

(The simplified character is found in the simplified character index under radical #14, 八.)

門 门 — mén (199) — door; gate

門 門

门 门

剩 — shèng (†) — to remain; left over

剩 丿 二 千 乖 乖 乘 剩

關 關 關

頭	头	tóu (75) head	
頭 豆 頭			
头 头			

及	及	jí (465) reach	
及 及			
及 及			

頭 頭 頭

Dialogue II

Character	Pinyin	No.	Meaning	Components
本	běn	(138)	M (for books)	本 木 本
如	rú	(145)	like; as if	如 女 如
果	guǒ	(223)	fruit; result	果 曰 果
罰 / 罚	fá	(†)	to fine; to punish	罰 罒 詈 罰 / 罚 罒 罚

(Note: The traditional character is found in the traditional radical index under radical #122, 网, *not* #109, 目; the simplified character is found in the simplified radical index under radical #120, 四.)

罰　罰　罰

續	续	xù (637) to continue; to extend	續	续	續	續				
see page 123		續	续		续	续				
續	糸	續								
续	纟	续								

必		bì (337) must	必	必			
		必					
必	丶	心	心	必	必		

須	须	xū (476) must	須	须	須	須				
		須	须		须	须			
須	彡	須							
须	彡	须							

典		diǎn (†) standard work	典	典			
		典					
典	丶	冂	曰	由	曲	曲	典

續   續   續

Fun With Characters

I. SEEK AND FIND.

Hidden in the box below are some words and phrases from the text. See how many you can find and circle them. Phrases can go horizontally left to right (→), vertically top to bottom (↓), or diagonally upper left to lower right (↘) or lower left to upper right (↗).

兩	盤	錄	音	帶	必	在	樓	下
可	卡	鐘	八	把	續	圖	分	如
以	星	期	六	學	借	書	證	進
借	過	果	頭	生	信	館	用	放
多	其	他	的	證	件	少	來	語
久	究	法	五	留	請	聽	職	言
開	到	幾	點	在	詞	字	識	實
小	上	館	關	這	忘	典	研	驗
辦	聲	時	門	兒	二	能	教	室

II. RADICAL IDENTIFICATION.

Provide the Pīnyīn for each of the following characters and put the radical component each set has in common in the parentheses to the right.

忘 ______	忙 ______	慣 (惯) ______	(____)
桌 ______	校 ______	樓 (楼) ______	(____)
悶 (闷) ______	開 (开) ______	關 (关) ______	(____)
實 (实) ______	續 (续) ______	賣 (卖) ______	(____)
證 (证) ______	罰 (罚) ______	讓 (让) ______	(____)

III. Matching.

First, draw a line connecting the Pīnyīn to its traditional character. Then, connect the traditional character to its simplified counterpart. Finally, draw a line connecting the simplified character to its English meaning.

Pīnyīn	Traditional	Simplified	English
dài	樓	门	floor; storey
fá	證	及	evidence
guān	帶	头	belt; tape
jí	職	关	duty; job
lóu	實	证	reality
mén	及	实	reach
shí	須	带	must
tóu	門	罚	door
xū	頭	须	head
xù	罰	验	to fine
yàn	關	职	to close
zhèng	驗	续	to examine
zhí	續	楼	to continue

IV. Fill in the Squares.

Fill in each of the empty squares below with one character each that contains the radical component provided.

	木	

	頁	

	人	

Dialogue I

運 运
yùn (301)
to carry; to transport
運 运
運 冖 軍 運
运 云 运

動 动
dòng (58)
to move; to stir
動 动
動 重 動
动 云 动

旁
páng (645)
side
旁
旁 亠 立 立 旁

遠 远
yuǎn (341)
far; distant; remote
遠 远
遠 袁 遠
远 元 远

動 動 動

		zhù (201) to live (at)	住			住	住			
住	亻	亻	住							

		lí (426) from; away	離	离		離	離			
see page 123						离	离			
離	文	产	卤	离	离	离	離			
离	文	产	卤	离	离	离				

		huó (88) to live	活			活	活			
活	氵	活								

		xīn (82) heart	心			心	心			
心	心									

		diàn (817) store; shop	店			店	店			
店	广	店								

田 (stroke order 1–5)

tián (727)
(a surname); field

田 田 田

金 (stroke order 1–8)

jīn (514)
(a surname); gold; metal

金 金 金

金 金 金

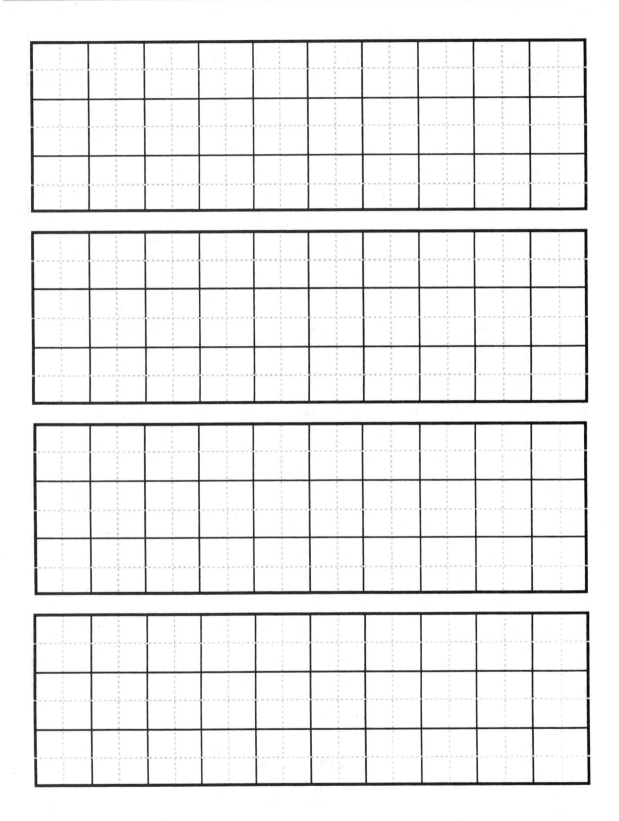

Dialogue II

城			chéng (528) city; town			城	城				
			城								
城	土	圹	圹	坊	城	城	城				

閉	闭		bì (†) to close			閉	閉				
			閉	闭		闭	闭				
閉	門	閉									
闭	门	闭									

著	着		zhe (18) P			著	著				
			著	着		着	着				
著	艹	著									
着	ⸯ	兰	羊	着							

眼			yǎn (148) eye			眼	眼				
			眼								
眼	目	眼									

著 著 着

睛		jīng (493) eyeball			睛	睛				
		睛								
睛	目	睛								

從	从	cóng (89) from			從	從				
		從	从		从	从				
從	ノ	彳	彳\'	彸	彸	䘸	從	從		
从	人	从								

直		zhí (274) straight			直	直				
		直	直	直△						
直	十	直								

往		wàng / wǎng (†) towards			往	往				
		往								
往	彳	往								

南		nán (456) south			南	南				
		南								
南	十	冂	冂	冂	南					

口		kǒu (182) mouth		口	口				
		口							
口	口								

拐		guǎi (†) to turn		拐	拐				
		拐	拐						
拐	扌	扌	拐						

哎	哎	āi (885) Excl.		哎	哎				
		哎	哎		哎	哎			
哎	口	口艹	哎						
哎	口	口艹	哎						

燈	灯	dēng (571) light; lamp		燈	燈				
		燈	灯		灯	灯			
燈	火	燈							
灯	火	灯							

燈   燈   燈

右		yòu (642) right	右	右

右 ナ 右

單	单	dān (501) one; single; odd	單	單
		單 单	单	单

單 口 吅 罒 單 單

单 丷 台 旦 单

左		zuǒ (575) left	左	左

左 ナ 左

面		miàn (68) face; side	面	面

面 而 而 面 面

京		jīng (†) capital	京	京

京 京

Fun With Characters

I. Crossword Puzzle.

Fill in the squares by providing translations for the cues given below.

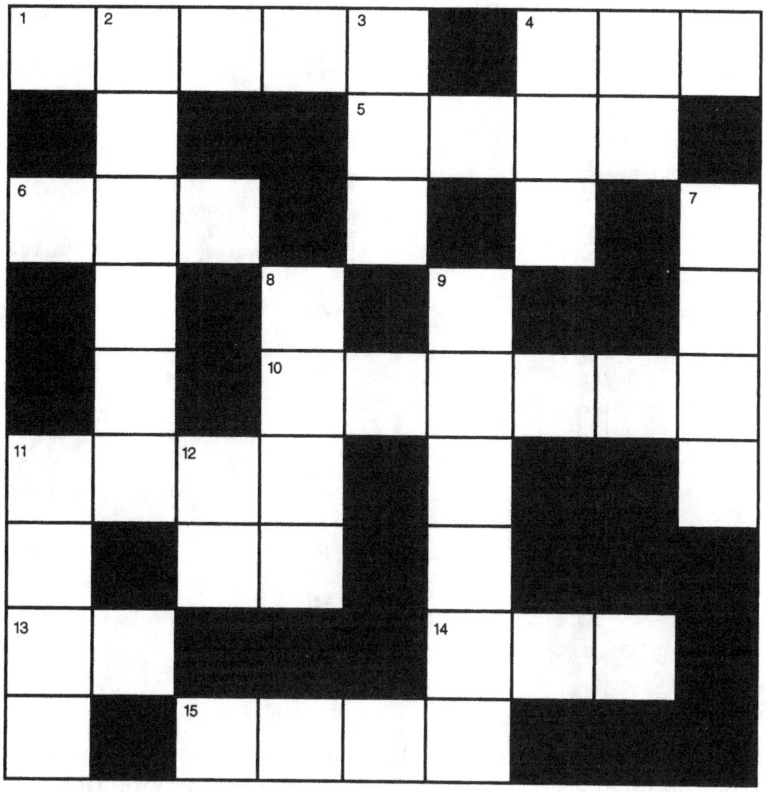

Across

1. Where are you going?
4. had I known earlier
5. students attend class
6. go with you
10. not studying new words is no good
11. what place
13. to ask directions
14. Chinatown
15. computer center

Down

2. What do you do in the morning?
3. go to school
4. Good morning.
7. take (lit., 'walk') a one-way street
8. very inconvenient
9. student activity center
12. map

II. Radical Identification.

Provide the Pīnyīn for each of the following characters and put the radical component each set has in common in the parentheses to the right.

眼	______	睛	______	看	______	(______)
把	______	拐	______	拌	______	(______)
功	______	拐	______	動 (动)	______	(______)
必	______	慢	______	悶 (闷)	______	(______)

III. Matching.

First, draw a line connecting the Pīnyīn to its traditional character. Then, connect the traditional character to its simplified counterpart. Finally, draw a line connecting the simplified character to its English meaning.

Pīnyīn	Traditional	Simplified	English
āi	離	着	to close
bì	燈	运	to move
cóng	遠	远	to transport
dān	運	离	away (from)
dēng	單	动	single
dòng	著	灯	light
lí	閉	单	from
yuǎn	動	从	Excl.
yùn	從	闭	far
zhe	哎	哎	P

IV. Phonological Distinction.

Provide the **full** Pīnyīn for each of the following characters and then put the basic homonym (initial + final, but no tone) each set shares in the parentheses to the right.

王	______	往	______	忘	______	(_____)
有	______	又	______	右	______	(_____)
昨	______	左	______	坐	______	(_____)
火	______	活	______	貨 (货)	______	(_____)
今	______	金	______	進 (进)	______	(_____)
京	______	睛	______	經 (经)	______	(_____)
南	______	男	______	難 (难)	______	(_____)
只	______	直	______	職 (职)	______	(_____)
李	______	裏 (里)	______	離 (离)	______	(_____)
者	______	著 (着)	______	這 (这)	______	(_____)

Dialogue I

表	biǎo (221) outside; form

Components: 表 龶 表

Note: Stroke #3 is a single vertical stroke. The dot shown above in the radical is provided as a reminder that the character is found under traditional radical #145 (simplified radical #147), 衣.

班	bān (703) class

Components: 班 王 玎 班

汁	zhī (†) juice

Components: 汁 氵 汁

接	jiē (279) to meet; to receive

Components: 接 扌 护 接

林	lín (721) (a surname); forest

Components: 林 木 林

Dialogue II

禮 (see page 123)	礼	lǐ (341) ceremony	禮 礼

禮 礻 礻 礻 礻 礻 禮

礼 礻 礼

物		wù (132) thing	物

物 牛 物

聰 (see page 123)	聪	cōng (†) acute hearing	聰 聪

聰 耳 耳 耳 聰 聰 聰

聪 耳 耳 耳 聪

暑		shǔ (†) heat; hot weather	暑

暑 日 暑

禮 禮 禮

長	长	zhǎng / cháng (100) to grow; to look / long	長	長			
長	长	長	长		长	长			
長	長								
长	长								

愛	爱	ài (312) to love	愛	愛			
愛	爱	愛	爱		爱	爱			
愛	一	兴	悉	愛					
爱	一	兴	爱						

屬	属	shǔ (†) to belong to	屬	屬			
屬	属	屬	属		屬	属			
屬	ㄱ	ㄱ	尸	尺	屌	屏	屠	屬	屬	屬	屬
	屬									
属	尸	尸	居	屌	属	属	属			

狗		gǒu (1000) dog	狗	狗			
狗				狗					
狗	ノ	犭	犭	狗					

鼻		bí (†) nose	鼻	鼻				
		鼻						
鼻	自	畠	畠	鼻	鼻			

嘴		zuǐ (520) mouth	嘴	嘴				
		嘴						
嘴	口	口此	咮	嘴	嘴	嘴		

將	将	jiāng (295) to be going to	將	將				
		將	将		將	将		
將	㇐	㇉	爿	爿	爿	將		
将	㇐	㇉	汋	将				

定		dìng (121) to decide; to fix; to set	定	定				
		定						
定	宀	定						

臉	脸	liǎn (365) face	臉	臉				
		臉	脸		臉	臉		
臉	月	臉						
脸	月	脸						

腿 腿
tuǐ (852)
leg

腿 月 月艮 腿
腿 月 月艮 腿

指
zhǐ (272)
finger

指 扌 扌匕 指

應 应
yīng (215)
should; ought to

see page 124

應 广 广亻 广隹 應
应 广 广丶 广丶丶 广丶丶丶 应

該 该
gāi (354)
should; ought to

該 言 該
该 讠 该

應 應 應

彈	弹	tán (698) to play			弹	弹				
		弹	弹		弹	弹				
彈	弓	彈								
弹	弓	弹								

鋼	钢	gāng (573) steel			鋼	鋼				
		鋼	钢		钢	钢				
鋼	金	鋼								
钢	钅	钢								

琴		qín (†) stringed instrument			琴	琴				
		琴								
琴	王	王王	琴							

倫	伦	lún (†) relationship			倫	倫				
		倫	伦		伦	伦				
倫	亻	伀	伶	伶	伶	倫	倫			
伦	亻	伀	伦							

姆

mǔ (女)

*nurse; *maid

姆 女 姆

姆 姆 姆

Fun With Characters

I. Seek and Find.

Hidden in the box below are some words and phrases from the text. See how many you can find and circle them. Phrases can go horizontally left to right (→), vertically top to bottom (↓), or diagonally upper left to lower right (↘) or lower left to upper right (↗).

祝	水	會	琴	以	喝	果	指	他
暑	過	長	得	真	可	愛	來	幾
祝	你	生	日	快	樂	海	一	歲
鼻	今	日	日	湯	又	女	腿	了
手	年	禮	姐	飯	聽	定	朋	該
應	多	物	做	到	明	説	兒	友
鋼	大	會	將	後	又	龍	猴	豬
汁	不	汽	舞	表	用	雞	屬	牛
我	在	看	書	呢	功	羊	馬	狗

II. Phonetic Identification.

Provide the Pīnyīn for each of the following characters and provide the "phonetic" ("sound radical/component") in the parentheses along with its Pīnyīn. The first one has been done for you.

校	xiào	餃 (饺)	jiǎo	(交	jiāo)
拌	______	胖	______	(______	______)
玩	______	完	______	(______	______)
空	______	紅 (红)	______	(______	______)
起	______	記 (记)	______	(______	______)
悶 (闷)	______	問 (问)	______	(______	______)
雖 (虽)	______	誰 (谁)	______	(______	______)

III. Matching.

First, draw a line connecting the Pīnyīn to its traditional character. Then, connect the traditional character to its simplified counterpart. Finally, draw a line connecting the simplified character to its English meaning.

Pīnyīn	Traditional	Simplified	English
ài	禮	长	to play
cháng	將	腿	to love
cōng	該	属	to grow
gāi	彈	弹	to belong to
gāng	屬	脸	to be going to
jiāng	長	爱	face
lǐ	臉	钢	long
liǎn	長	将	should
lún	應	该	ceremony
shǔ	鋼	应	acute hearing
tán	腿	伦	relationship
tuǐ	聰	礼	should
yīng	倫	聪	steel
zhǎng	愛	长	leg

IV. Fill in the Squares.

Fill in each of the empty squares below with one character each that contains the radical component provided.

	亻	

	扌	

	广	

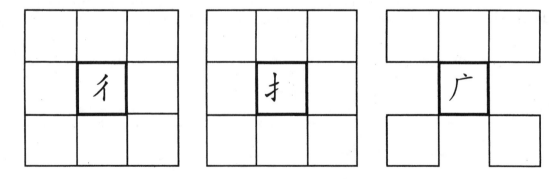

Dialogue I

病			bìng (424) illness	病	病			
			病					
病	广	广	疒	疒	病	病			

肚			dù (†) stomach; belly	肚	肚			
			肚					
肚	月	肚						

疼			téng (†) to be painful	疼	疼			
			疼					
疼	疒	疼						

死			sǐ (356) to die	死	死			
			死					
死	一	歹	死					

廁 厕			cè (†) lavatory; toilet; W.C.	廁	廁			
			廁	厕	厕	厕		
廁	广	厠	廁					
厕	厂	厕	厕					

躺

tǎng (†)

to lie down

躺 身 身' 躺 躺

檢 检

jiǎn (768)

to inspect; to examine

檢 木 檢

检 木 检

查

chá (†)

to inspect; to examine

查 木 杳 查

壞 坏

see page 144

huài (544)

bad

壞 土 圹 坜 壞 壞

坏 土 坏

壞 壞 壞

Traditional	Simplified	Pinyin	No.	Meaning
針	针	zhēn	*(771)*	needle
種	种	zhǒng / zhòng	*(86)*	kind; type
藥	药	yào	*(629)*	medicine

針 金 針

针 钅 针

種 禾 種

种 禾 种

藥 *see page 144*

藥 艹 … 藥

药 艹 … 药

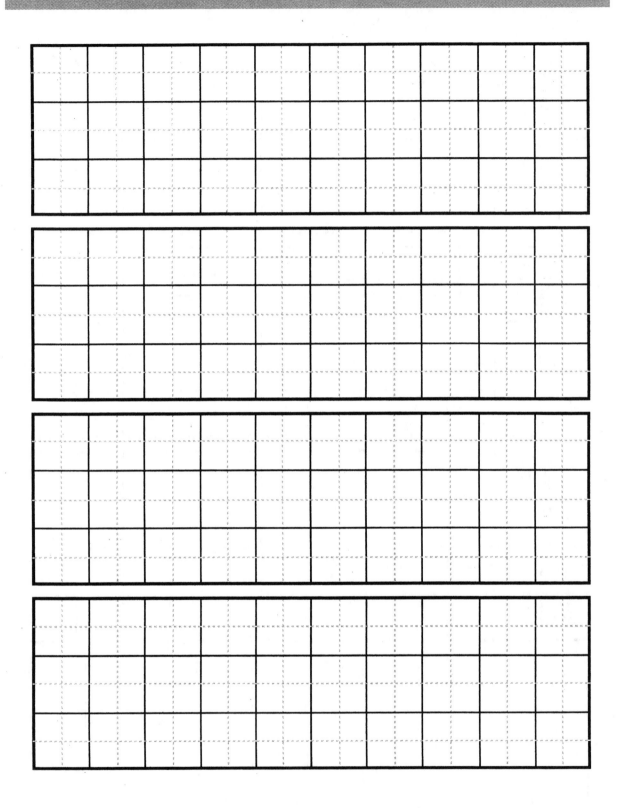

Dialogue II

淚 泪		lèi (964) tear 淚 泪		淚 淚			
淚	氵	氵	沪	淚			
泪	氵	泪					

| 流 | | liú (278) to flow; to shed 流 | | 流 流 | | | |
| 流 | 氵 | 氵 | 汸 | 泞 | 济 | 流 | |

| 身 | | shēn (155) body 身 | | 身 身 | | | |
| 身 | 身 | | | | | | |

體 体 see page 144		tǐ (191) body 體 体		體 體 體 体 体 体			
體	冂	口	冎	骨	骨	體	體
体	亻	体					

癢	痒	yǎng (†) to itch
癢	痒	

see page 125

癢 疒 … 癢

痒 疒 … 痒

敏	mǐn (†) quick; nimble; agile
敏	

敏 每 敏

拿	ná (327) to hold; to take
拿	

拿 人 亼 合 拿

趕	赶	gǎn (504) hurry; rush
趕	赶	

趕 走 起 趕

赶 走 赶

癢 癢 癢

越		yuè (382) exceed; overlap	越	越			
		越					
越	走	走	起	赿	越	越	

重		zhòng (153) serious; heavy	重	重			
		重					
重	重						

健	健	jiàn (†) healthy; strong	健	健			
		健	健	健	健		
健	亻	伊	健				
健	亻	伊	健				

康		kāng (†) well-being; health	康	康			
		康					
康	广	庐	庐	庚	康		

保		bǎo (400) to protect; to defend	保	保			
		保					
保	亻	仔	保				

險 险

xiǎn (†)

danger; risk

險 险

險 阝 險

险 阝 险

猜

cāi (†)

to guess

猜

猜 犭 猜

馬 马

mǎ (359)

(a surname); horse

馬 马

馬 馬

马 马

馬 馬 馬

Fun With Characters

I. Crossword Puzzle.

Fill in the squares by providing translations for the cues given below.

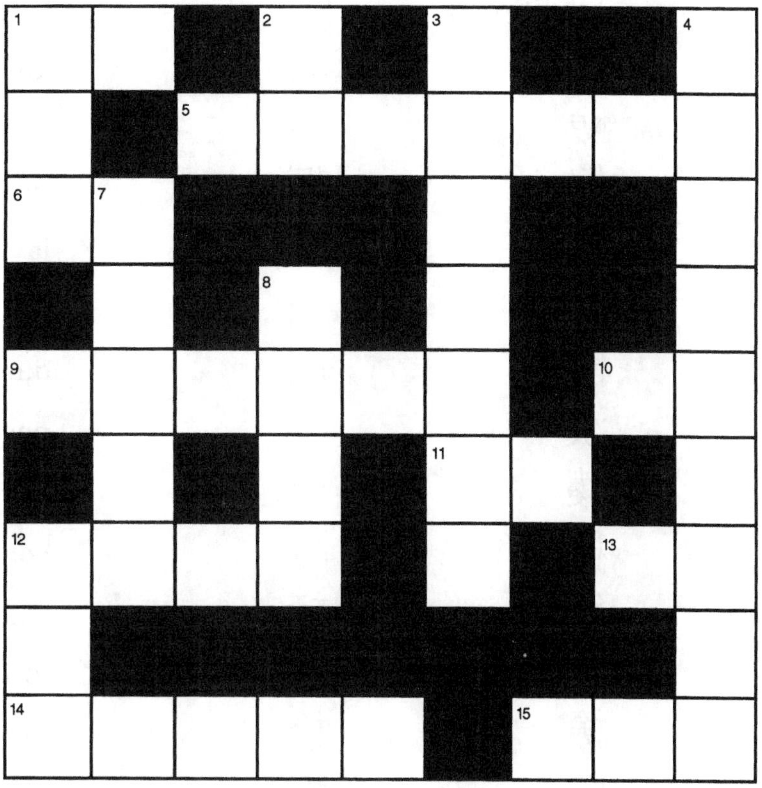

Across

1. Seeing a Doctor
5. These medications are all useless.
6. to get sick
9. My stomach is uncomfortable.
10. spend money
11. expired
12. legs hurt terribly
13. together
14. grown to be very pretty
15. guessed correctly

Down

1. to see a doctor
2. those
3. He is also allergic to clothing.
4. I picked up the money with my hands. (把)
7. The patient has a stomachache.
8. She doesn't itch (anymore).
12. legs are very long

II. Radical Identification.

Provide the Pīnyīn for each of the following characters and put the radical component each set has in common in the parentheses to the right.

起 ______	越 ______	趕 (赶) ______	(_____)
地 ______	城 ______	壞 (坏) ______	(_____)
票 ______	視 (视) ______	禮 (礼) ______	(_____)
鋼 (钢) ______	鐘 (钟) ______	針 (针) ______	(_____)

III. Matching.

First, draw a line connecting the Pīnyīn to its traditional character. Then, connect the traditional character to its simplified counterpart. Finally, draw a line connecting the simplified character to its English meaning.

Pīnyīn	Traditional	Simplified	English
cè	馬	马	kind; type
gǎn	險	体	tear(drop)
huài	健	坏	medicine
jiǎn	趕	针	lavatory
jiàn	癢	泪	healthy
lèi	體	厕	danger
mǎ	淚	种	needle
tǐ	藥	药	horse
xiǎn	種	险	body
yǎng	針	赶	bad
yào	壞	健	to itch
zhēn	檢	检	to rush
zhǒng	廁	痒	to inspect

IV. Phonological Distinction.

Provide the **full** Pīnyīn for each of the following characters and then put the basic homonym (initial + final, but no tone) each set shares in the parentheses to the right.

四	______	死	______	思	______	(_____)
六	______	流	______	留	______	(_____)
中	______	重	______	種 (种)	______	(_____)
糖	______	躺	______	湯 (汤)	______	(_____)
睛	______	精	______	經 (经)	______	(_____)
動	______	東 (东)	______	懂 (懂)	______	(_____)
媽 (妈)	______	馬 (马)	______	嗎 (吗)	______	(_____)

Dialogue I

參	参	cān ˋ (564) to participate	参	参			
		参	参		参	参	
参	ㄥ	ㄥ	ㄥㄥ	矢	参		
参	ㄥ	矢	参				

加		jiā (189) to add	加	加			
		加					
加	力	加					

印		yìn (812) seal; stamp	印	印			
		印					
印	ˊ	㇈	㇏	印			

象	象	xiàng (107) appearance	象	象			
		象	象		象	象	
象	ㄅ	臽	象				
象	ㄅ	臽	象				

演		yǎn (778) to show; to perform	演	演			
		演					
演	㇒	沪	沪	浐	漄	漄	演

費 费

fèi (756)

to spend; to take (effort)

費 费

力

lì (119)

power; strength

力

倆 俩

liǎ (†)

M; two (people)

倆 俩

倆 亻 倆

俩 亻 俩

費 費 費

Dialogue II

碼	码	mǎ (†) number

碼	石	碼	
码	石	码	

劇	剧	jù (†) play; opera

劇	丨	⺊	上	卢	虍	豦	劇
剧	尸	居	剧				

慶	庆	qìng (†) to celebrate

see page 125

慶	广	户					慶
庆	广	庆					

掃	扫	sǎo (†) to sweep

掃	扌			扫		掃
扫	扌			扫		

房 房		fáng (440) house; room	房	房			
		戶 房	房	房			
房	一	尸	房					
房	丶	尸	房					

整		zhěng (395) neat; tidy	整	整			
		整					
整	束	敕	整					

理		lǐ (133) to tidy up; put in order	理	理			
		理					
理	王	理						

旅		lǚ (†) to travel	旅	旅			
		旅					
旅	方	扩	扩	旅	旅	旅		

係 系		xì (268) connection	係	係			
		係 系	系	系			
係	亻	亻	係					
系	一	系						

紐 纽

niǔ (+)

button

紐 纽

紐 紐 費

Fun With Characters

I. Seek and Find.

Hidden in the box below are some words and phrases from the text. See how many you can find and circle them. Phrases can go horizontally left to right (→), vertically top to bottom (↓), or diagonally upper left to lower right (↘) or lower left to upper right (↗).

買	慶	祝	慶	祝	中	打	約	會
哪	得	參	氣	一	整	國	了	得
一	活	到	來	號	言	極	電	紐
位	理	起	好	李	好	為	掃	影
天	不	歌	王	友	印	房	定	子
想	碼	王	朋	很	喜	歡	李	友
算	旅	好	很	漂	你	有	空	嗎
象	了	白	帥	亮	力	著	記	劇
成	家	吧	我	請	你	吃	晚	飯

II. Phonetic Identification.

Provide the Pīnyīn for each of the following characters and provide the "phonetic" ("sound radical/component") in the parentheses along with its Pīnyīn. The first two have been done for you.

檢 (检)	jiǎn	險 (险)	xiǎn	(僉 (佥)	qiān)
躺	tǎng	常	cháng	(尚	shàng)
放	______	房 (房)	______	(______	______)
懂 (懂)	______	種 (种)	______	(______	______)
媽 (妈)	______	碼 (码)	______	(______	______)
臉 (脸)	______	驗 (验)	______	(______	______)

III. Matching.

First, draw a line connecting the Pīnyīn to its traditional character. Then, connect the traditional character to its simplified counterpart. Finally, draw a line connecting the simplified character to its English meaning.

Pīnyīn	Traditional	Simplified	English
cān	費	象	appearance
fáng	象	剧	button
fèi	參	费	connection
jù	倆	俩	house
liǎ	碼	钮	number
mǎ	劇	参	play
niǔ	慶	码	two (people)
qìng	掃	房	to celebrate
sǎo	房	系	to participate
xì	係	庆	to spend
xiàng	鈕	扫	to sweep

IV. Fill in the Squares.

Fill in each of the empty squares below with one character each that contains the radical component provided.

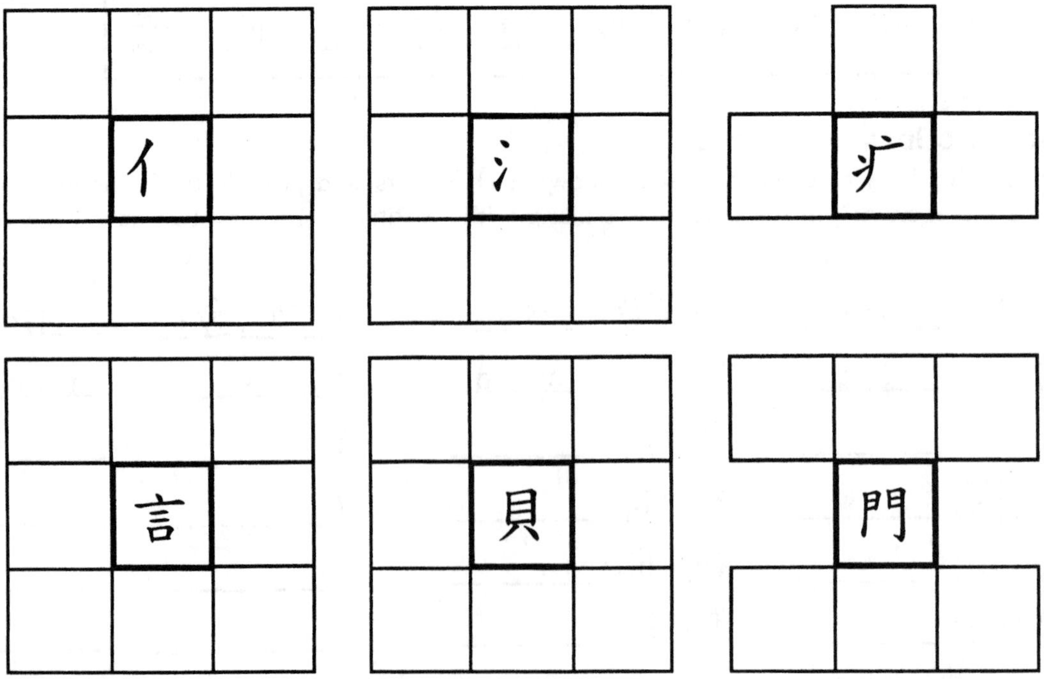

Narrative

		chǎo (†) noisy	吵	吵				
吵		吵						
吵	口	吵						

連	连	lián (328) even	連	連				
		連 连	连	连				
連	車	連						
连	车	连						

準	准	zhǔn (404) accurate	準	準				
		準 准	准	准				
準	氵	淮	準					
准	冫	准						

備	备	bèi (432) to prepare	備	備				
		備 备	备	备				
備	亻	伊	伊	備				
备	丿	夂	备					

搬

bān (†)

to move

搬 扌 搬

紙 纸

zhǐ (623)

paper

紙 糸 糹 糺 紅 紙

纸 纟 纟 纟 纸 纸

廣 广

guǎng (524)

broad; vast

廣 广 廣

广 广

附 附

fù (†)

get close to; be near to

附 阝 附

附 阝 附

Character	Pinyin	No.	Meaning
寓	yù	(†)	to reside; to live (at)
里	lǐ	(26)	*li* (a unit of length)
套	tào	(524)	set / suite
卧 / 臥	wò	(†)	to lie (down)
廚 / 厨	chú	(†)	kitchen

see page 125

傢	家	jiā (†) *furniture	傢 家	
傢	亻	伫	傢	
家	宀	家		

俱	具	jù (450) all; complete	俱 具	
俱	亻	俱		
具	具			

俱 俱 俱

Dialogue

沙		shā (649) sand 沙	沙	沙			
沙	氵	沙					

椅		yǐ (†) chair 椅	椅	椅			
椅	木	杶	椅				

架		jià (806) frame; shelf 架	架	架			
架	加	架					

安		ān (†) peaceful; quiet 安	安	安			
安	宀	安					

靜	静	jìng (597) quiet; calm 靜 静	靜	靜			
靜	青	靑	靗	靜			
静	青	靑	静	静			

非		fēi (497) not; no	非	非			
		非	非				
非	ノ ナ ヺ ヺ ヺ 非						

元		yuán (776) *yuan* (Chn dollar)	元	元			
		元					
元	二 元						

押		yā (†) to pawn; give as security	押	押			
		押					
押	扌 扣 押						

當	当	dāng (130) to serve as; to be	當	當			
		當	当	当	当		
當	凸 當						
当	⺌ 当 当 当						

許	许	xǔ (256) to allow; to be allowed	許	許			
		許	许	許	许		
許	言 許						
许	讠 许						

養 养

yǎng (624)

to raise

養 养

養 养

養 養 養

Fun With Characters

I. Crossword Puzzle.

Fill in the squares by providing translations for the cues given below.

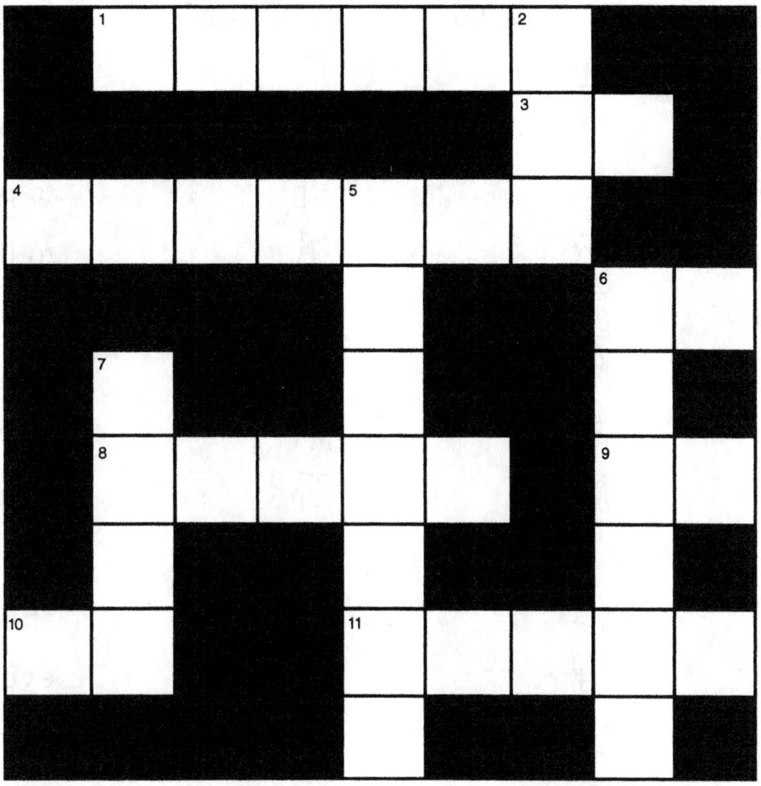

Across

1. one month's rent
3. landlord
4. dining table with four chairs
6. inexpensive
8. the room has a desk
9. pay money
10. living room
11. give him a call

Down

2. rent a room/house
5. return that book to me
6. no need to pay water and electricity fees
7. one bedroom and one living room

II. Radical Identification.

Provide the Pīnyīn for each of the following characters and put the radical component each set has in common in the parentheses to the right.

押	______	搬	______	拿	______	(_____)
架	______	椅	______	林	______	(_____)
素	______	紙 (纸)	______	灣 (湾)	______	(_____)
倆 (俩)	______	係 (系)	______	臥 (卧)	______	(_____)

III. Matching.

First, draw a line connecting the Pīnyīn to its traditional character. Then, connect the traditional character to its simplified counterpart. Finally, draw a line connecting the simplified character to its English meaning.

Pīnyīn	Traditional	Simplified	English
bèi	連	广	to serve as
chú	準	当	to raise
dāng	備	许	to prepare
fù	紙	纸	to lie (down)
guǎng	廣	连	to be near to
jiā	附	具	to allow
jìng	臥	附	quiet
jù	廚	卧	paper
lián	傢	备	kitchen
wò	俱	养	*furniture
xǔ	靜	准	even
yǎng	當	家	broad
zhǐ	許	厨	all; complete
zhǔn	養	静	accurate

IV. Phonological Distinction.

Provide the **full** Pīnyīn for each of the following characters and then put the basic homonym (initial + final, but no tone) each set shares in the parentheses to the right.

一	______	意	______	椅	______	(______)
雨	______	寓	______	魚 (鱼)	______	(______)
北	______	杯	______	備 (备)	______	(______)
架	______	家	______	傢 (家)	______	(______)
只	______	職 (职)	______	紙 (纸)	______	(______)
元	______	園 (园)	______	遠 (远)	______	(______)

Dialogue I

郵	邮	yóu (†) mail; post	郵	郵			
		郵 邮	邮	邮			
郵	垂	郵					
邮	由	邮					

局		jú (594) office; bureau	局	局			
		局					
局	尸	弓	局				

寄		jì (†) to mail; to send by mail	寄	寄			
		寄					
寄	宀	寄					

營	营	yíng (†) to operate; to run	營	營			
		營 营	营	营			
營	火	炏	燚	營	營	營	
营	艹	芦	营	营			

郵　　　邮　　　郵

貼 贴	tiē (†) to paste on; to stick on	貼 贴	
貼	貝	貼	
贴	贝	贴	

掛 挂	guà (877) to hang	掛 挂	
掛	扌	挂	掛
挂	扌	扗	挂

另	lìng (660) other	另	
另	口	另	

貼 貼 貼

Dialogue II

首		shǒu	(563)	head
首	丷	首		

飾	饰	shì	(†)	decorations
飾	食	飠	飾	
饰	饣	饣	饰	

鮮	鲜	xiān	(946)	fresh
鮮	魚	魚	鮮	鮮
鲜	鱼	鱼	鲜	鲜

束		shù	(967)	M; a bunch of (flowers)
束	束			

鮮 鮮 鮮

訂	订	dìng　(†) to order; to subscribe to		訂	订		
		訂	订		訂	订		
訂	言	訂						
订	讠	订						

收		shōu　(428) to receive		收	收		
		收					
收	丩	收					

存		cún　(630) to store; to keep		存	存		
		存					
存	才	存					

支		zhī　(498) to pay out		支	支		
		支					
支	十	支					

它		tā　(113) it		它	它		
		它					
它	宀	它					

民		mín (67) people	民 民
幣	币	bì (†) currency	幣 币
銀	银	yín (856) silver	銀 银

(Note: In the traditional character, strokes 1 and 6 are two separate strokes.)

幣 幣 幣

Fun With Characters

I. Seek and Find.

Hidden in the box below are some words and phrases from the text. See how many you can find and circle them. Phrases can go horizontally left to right (→), vertically top to bottom (↓), or diagonally upper left to lower right (↘) or lower left to upper right (↗).

在	北	京	的	郵	局	支	票	營
台	首	收	錢	這	存	郵	美	元
灣	手	塊	險	那	的	人	金	員
的	三	定	外	錢	離	越	民	海
郵	上	服	少	中	國	銀	行	幣
局	平	多	務	次	月	越	會	留
重	貼	張	業	裡	把	明	現	學
要	保	晚	寄	掛	號	快	信	生
麼	南	花	最	新	鮮	都	是	片

II. Radical Identification.

Provide the Pīnyīn for each of the following characters and put the radical component each set has in common in the parentheses to the right.

好 _____	孩 _____	存 _____	(_____)
另 _____	加 _____	助 _____	(_____)
鼻 _____	首 _____	道 (道) _____	(_____)
餐 _____	養 (养) _____	飾 (饰) _____	(_____)
說 (说) _____	許 (许) _____	訂 (订) _____	(_____)

III. MATCHING.

First, draw a line connecting the Pīnyīn to its traditional character. Then, connect the traditional character to its simplified counterpart. Finally, draw a line connecting the simplified character to its English meaning.

Pīnyīn	Traditional	Simplified	English
bì	郵	币	mail; post
dìng	營	订	to operate
guà	銀	挂	silver
shì	鮮	饰	fresh
tiē	貼	贴	to paste on
xiān	飾	鲜	decorations
yín	掛	银	to hang
yíng	訂	营	to order
yóu	幣	邮	currency

IV. FILL IN THE SQUARES.

Fill in each of the empty squares below with one character each that contains the radical component provided.

	氵	

	宀	

	阝	

(either on the left or the right side)

	巾	

	食	

	匕	

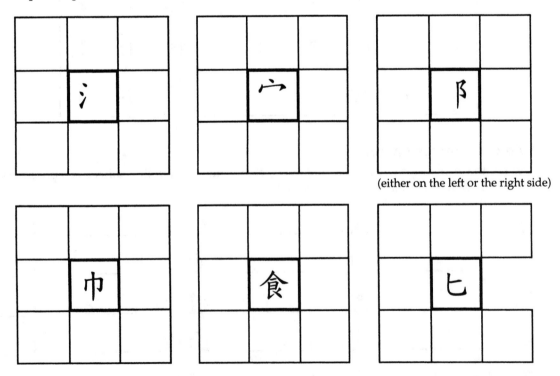

Dialogue I

胖		pàng　　　　　(†) fat	胖	胖			
		胖					
胖	月	胖					

怕		pà　　　　　(330) to fear; to be afraid	怕	怕			
		怕					
怕	忄	怕					

簡	简	jiǎn　　　　　(656) simple	簡	簡			
		簡	简	简	简		
簡	⺮	简	簡				
简	⺮	竹	简				

跑		pǎo　　　　　(369) to run	跑	跑			
		跑					
跑	𧾷	𧾷	趵	趵	趵	跑	

受		shòu　　　　　(330) to bear; to receive	受	受			
		受					
受	爫	受					

網 网	wǎng (†) net			網	網			
	網	网		网	网			
網	糸	紀	約	紀	網	網		
网	冂	冈	网					

拍	pāi (972) racket; to slap			拍	拍			
	拍							
拍	扌	拍						

籃 籃	lán (†) basket			籃	籃			
see page 125	籃	篮		籃	籃			
籃	⺮	管	篏	籃				
篮	⺮	竹	笁	篮				

游	yóu (676) to swim			游	游			
	游							
游	氵	汸	游	游				

籃   籃   籃

泳		yǒng (†) to swim	泳	泳
		泳		

泳 氵 氵 汀 汸 泳 泳

危		wēi (801) danger; peril	危	危
		危		

危 ⺈ 厃 𠂊 危 危

淹		yān (†) to flood; to submerge	淹	淹
		淹		

淹 氵 汏 淹

願	愿	yuàn (577) be willing	願	願
		願 愿	愿	愿

願 厂 后 原 願

愿 厂 后 原 愿

願 願 願

Dialogue II

提		tí (231) to raise; to carry	提
提	扌	扌日	提

調	调	tiáo / diào (479) to change; to mix; adjust	調 调
調	言	訁冂	訁冂土	調
调	讠	讠冂	讠冂土	调

足		zú (758) foot	足
足	口	足	

賽	赛	sài (†) game; match; competition	賽 赛
賽	宀	実	賽
赛	宀	実	赛

圓	圆	yuán (941) round	圓	圆
圓	冂	圓	圓	
圆	冂	圆	圆	

際	际	jì (480) border; edge	際	际
際	阝	阝	陊	際
际	阝	际		

式		shì (540) style; type	式	
式	一	工	式	

腳	脚	jiǎo (484) foot	腳	脚
腳	月	脟	腳	
脚	月	胠	脚	

踢		tī　　　　　　(†) to kick　　　　踢	踢	踢			
踢	𧾷	踢					

手		shǒu　　　　(115) hand　　　　手	手	手			
手	手						

抱		bào　　　　(838) to hold; to hug　　抱	抱	抱			
抱	扌	抱					

壓 压 *see page 125*		yā　　　　(511) to crush; to press down 壓　压	壓 压	壓 压			
壓	厂	戸	肙	猒	壓		
压	厂	圧	压				

壓　　壓　　壓

被 — bèi (242) Preposition

被 衤 衤 衤 衤 被

擔 担 — dān (696) to carry (on a shoulder)

擔 扌 扌 扌 扌 擔

担 扌 扣 担

棒 — bàng (†) strong; good

棒 木 木 様 棒

特 — tè (326) special; particular

特 牛 特

傷 伤 — shāng (667) to injure; to hurt

傷 亻 亻 亻 傷

伤 亻 亻 伤

輸 输

shū (†)

to lose (a game, etc.)

輸	車	車人	車亼	車俞	輸
输	车	车人	车亼	车俞	输

贏 赢

see page 125

yíng (†)

to win (a game, etc.)

贏	亡	亡口	亡口月	亡口月貝	亡口月貝	贏	贏
赢	亡	亡口	亡口月	亡口月贝	亡口月贝	赢	赢

輸 輸 輸

贏 贏 贏

Fun With Characters

I. Crossword Puzzle.

Fill in the squares by providing translations for the cues given below.

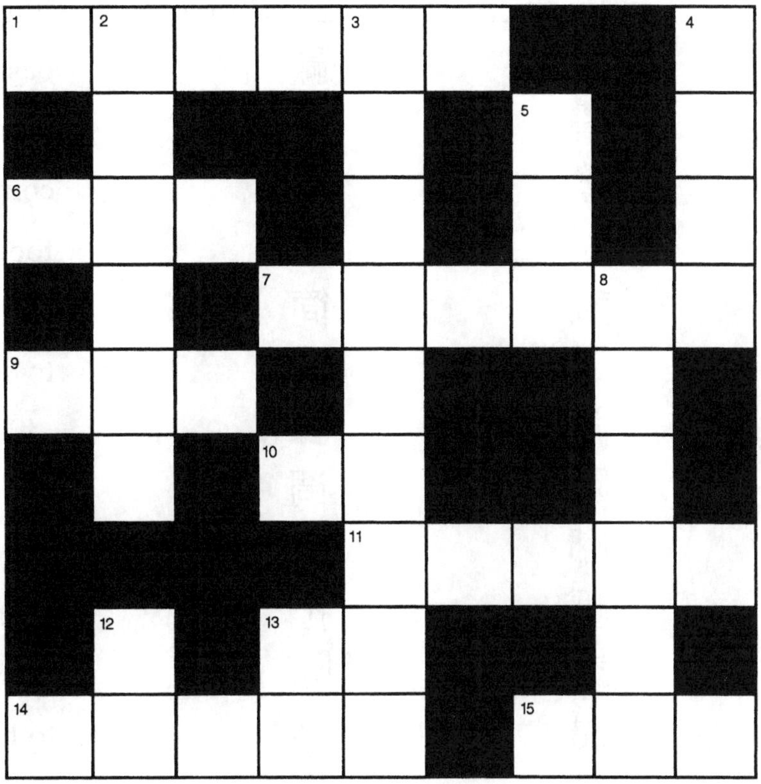

Across

1. Do you want to play with me?
6. don't spend money
7. (your) stomach then will get smaller
9. a lot of people
10. come in
11. fatter and fatter
13. too big
14. tennis is too expensive
15. let's go back

Down

2. no need to spend a lot of money
3. My belly is getting bigger and bigger.
4. was crushed
5. I can't
8. Young Lin will keep getting fatter.
12. soccer
13. too expensive

II. Radical Identification.

Provide the Pīnyīn for each of the following characters and put the radical component each set has in common in the parentheses to the right.

路	______	跑	______	踢	______	(_____)
游	______	泳	______	淹	______	(_____)
胖	______	腐	______	腳 (脚)	______	(_____)
連 (连)	______	運 (运)	______	輸 (输)	______	(_____)

III. Matching.

First, draw a line connecting the Pīnyīn to its traditional character. Then, connect the traditional character to its simplified counterpart. Finally, draw a line connecting the simplified character to its English meaning.

Pīnyīn	Traditional	Simplified	English
dān	簡	赢	basket
jì	網	篮	border
jiǎn	籃	赛	competition
jiǎo	願	愿	foot
lán	調	简	net
sài	賽	输	to win
shāng	圓	脚	to lose
shū	際	调	to injure
tiáo	腳	圆	to crush
wǎng	壓	担	to carry
yā	擔	际	to adjust
yíng	傷	网	to be willing
yuán	輸	伤	round
yuàn	贏	压	simple

IV. Phonological Distinction.

Provide the **full** Pīnyīn for each of the following characters and then put the basic homonym (initial + final, but no tone) each set shares in the parentheses to the right.

手	______	收	______	受	______	(_____)
叫	______	教	______	腳 (脚)	______	(_____)
押	______	呀	______	壓 (压)	______	(_____)
北	______	被	______	貝 (贝)	______	(_____)
跳	______	調 (调)	______	條 (条)	______	(_____)
見	______	簡 (简)	______	檢 (检)	______	(_____)
員	______	圓 (圆)	______	願 (愿)	______	(_____)

Dialogue I

計 计

jì (322)

to count; to compute

計 计

計 言 計

计 讠 计

劃 划

huà (599)

to plan; to delimit

劃 划

劃 聿 書 畫 劃

划 戈 划

各

gè (204)

each; every

各

各 夂 各

護 护

see page 126

hù (625)

to protect

護 护

護 言 訁艹 謢 護

护 扌 扌丶 护

護 護 護

簽	签	qiān (†) to sign
簽	⺮	簽
签	⺮	签

航		háng (†) boat; ship; to navigate
航	舟	舟	舟	航

司		sī (816) to manage; to attend to
司	𠃌	司	司

減	减	jiǎn (835) to reduce; to decrease
減	氵	氵	氵	沍	減	減	減
减	冫	冫	冫	冱	减	减	减

簽 簽 簽

價 价

jià (647)

price; value

價 亻 㑱 價

价 亻 仒 价

社

shè (137)

community; society

社 礻 社

程

chéng (416)

rule; order; journey

程 禾 和 程

折

zhé (†)

to break; to discount

折 扌 折

價 價 價

頓	顿	dùn (†) M (for meals)			頓	頓			
		頓	顿		顿	顿			
頓	一	屯	由	頓					
顿	一	屯	由	顿					

華 see page 126	华	huá (†) magnificent; China			華	華			
		華	华		华	华			
華	艹	艹	芢	芢	莁	莲	華		
华	化	华							

華   華   華

Dialogue II

		chū (680) first; beginning		初	初			
初			初					
初	衤	初						

		qiān (407) thousand		千	千			
千			千	千				
千	丿	千						

		zhuǎn (343) to turn		轉	轉			
轉	转		轉	转		转	转	
see page 126								
轉	車	轉						
转	车	转						

		nèi (246) inside		內	內			
內	内		內	內		內	內	
內	冂	內						
內	冂	內						

轉   轉   轉

漲	涨	zhǎng (†)		涨	涨				
		to rise							
		涨	涨		涨	涨			
漲	氵	漲							
涨	氵	涨							

盛		shèng (†)		盛	盛				
		flourishing; abundant							
		盛			盛				
盛	成	盛							

韓	韩	hán (†)		韓	韓				
		(a surname); Korea							
		韓	韩		韩	韩			
韓	十	百	𠦝	軺	韓	韓	韓	韓	
韩	十	百	卓	𮢺	韩				

芝	芝	zhī (†)		芝	芝				
		*sesame (seed)							
		芝	芝		芝	芝			
芝	艹	芝							
芝	艹	芝							

韓   韓   韓

洛

luò (†)
(name of a river)

洛 | 氵 | 洛

杉

shān (†)
China fir

杉 | 木 | 杉

磯 矶

jī (†)
a rock in water; jetty

磯 | 石 | 磯
矶 | 石 | 矶

香

xiāng (959)
fragrant

香 | 禾 | 香

港

gǎng (†)
port; harbor

港 | 氵 | [illegible] | 洪 | [illegible] | [illegible] | 港

Fun With Characters

I. Seek and Find.

Hidden in the box below are some words and phrases from the text. See how many you can find and circle them. Phrases can go horizontally left to right (→), vertically top to bottom (↓), or diagonally upper left to lower right (↘) or lower left to upper right (↗).

轉	漲	一	邊	教	英	文	劃	有
六	六	邊	言	國	照	計	盛	的
加	月	學	減	為	麼	磯	日	有
香	初	中	華	什	定	折	證	有
洛	台	文	有	錢	航	旅	行	的
直	價	你	塊	簽	了	空	算	沒
程	飛	多	杉	煩	芝	韓	公	有
班	千	漢	痲	打	護	社	哥	司
一	頓	太	城	單	來	回	票	港

II. Radical Identification.

Provide the Pīnyīn for each of the following characters and put the radical component each set has in common in the parentheses to the right.

初 _____	被 _____	表 _____	(_____)
港 _____	漲 (涨) _____	減 (减) _____	(_____)
香 _____	簡 (简) _____	韓 (韩) _____	(_____)
張 (张) _____	漲 (涨) _____	灣 (湾) _____	(_____)
價 (价) _____	傷 (伤) _____	簽 (签) _____	(_____)

III. Matching.

First, draw a line connecting the Pīnyīn to its traditional character. Then, connect the traditional character to its simplified counterpart. Finally, draw a line connecting the simplified character to its English meaning.

Pīnyīn	Traditional	Simplified	English
dùn	磯	计	China
hán	芝	价	Korea
hù	韓	华	price
huá	漲	芝	rock in water
huà	轉	划	to reduce
jī	華	护	to count
jì	頓	矶	to plan
jià	價	转	to sign
jiǎn	減	顿	to rise
qiān	簽	涨	to turn
zhǎng	護	减	to protect
zhī	劃	韩	M (for meals)
zhuǎn	計	签	*sesame

IV. Fill in the Squares.

Fill in each of the empty squares below with one character each that contains the radical component provided.

	禾	

	示	

	艹	

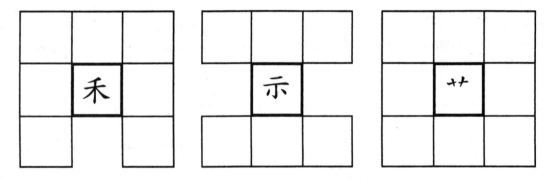

Dialogue I

父

fù (614)
father

父 八 父

母

mǔ (472)
mother

母 ㇄ 𠃑 母 母 母

Note: This character is found under traditional radical #80 (simplified radical #109), 毋.

婆

pó (†)
old woman

婆 氵 波 婆

阿 阿

ā (†)
Prefix

阿 阝 阿

阿 阝 阿

姨

yí (†)
aunt

姨 女 女 妇 姨

親 / 亲	qīn	*(241)*
	related by blood	
親 亲 親		
亲 亲		

戚	qī	*(†)*
	relative	
戚 一 厂 厈 戽 戚 戚 戚		

伯	bó	*(†)*
	uncle	
伯 亻 伯		

市	shì	*(461)*
	city; market	
市 亠 市		

親　　親　　親

鄉	乡	xiāng (634) countryside
		鄉 乡

鄉	∠	幺	乡	𨛜	鄉
乡	∠	幺	乡		

啦		lā (†) P
		啦

啦	口	吋	啦

鎮	镇	zhèn (990) town
		鎮 镇 鎭Δ

鎮	釒	鎮
镇	钅	镇

座		zuò (694) M (for bridges, mountains)
		座

座	广	广从	座

鎮 鎮 鎮

山		shān (193) mountain	山	山
		山		

山	山

河		hé (360) river	河	河
		河		

河	氵	河

樹	树	shù (401) tree	樹	樹
		樹 树	树	树

樹	木	梪	樹
树	木	权	树

滿	满	mǎn (349) full	滿	滿
		滿 满	满	满

滿	氵	汫	㴋	㴋	㴋	滿
满	氵	汫	满			

樹 樹 樹

風 风	fēng (262) wind	風 风
風 丿 几 凡 風		
风 丿 几 风		

景	jǐng (811) scenery; scene	景
景 日 景		

季	jì (987) season	季 季
季 禾 季		

滑	huá (†) to slide	滑
滑 氵 滑		

風 風 風

雪	雪	xuě (627) snow	雪 雪

雪	雨	雪
雪	雨	雪

迎	迎	yíng (958) to welcome	迎 迎

迎	丿	𠂎	卬	迎
迎	丿	𠂎	卬	迎

州		zhōu (†) state	州

州	丶	丿	丿	州	州	州

舊 see page 126	旧	jiù (622) old	舊 旧

舊	艹	雈	舊
旧	丨	旧	

Dialogue II

政 zhèng (196) politics

治 zhì (316) to rule; to control

濟 济 jì (368) to help; to benefit

化 huà (143) to change

部	部	bù (117) part; section	部 部
部	立	音	部
部	立	音	部

差	差	chà (722) lacking; short of; less	差 差
差	羊	羊	差
差	羊	差	

颳	刮	guā (†) to blow	颳 刮
颳	風	颳	
刮	舌	刮	

導	导	dǎo (265) to lead; to guide	導 导
導	道	導	
导	巳	导	

see page 126

遊	游	yóu (†) to travel; to tour	遊	游
遊	斿	遊		
游	氵	游		

遊 遊 遊

Fun With Characters

I. Crossword Puzzle.

Fill in the squares by providing translations or answers for the cues given below.

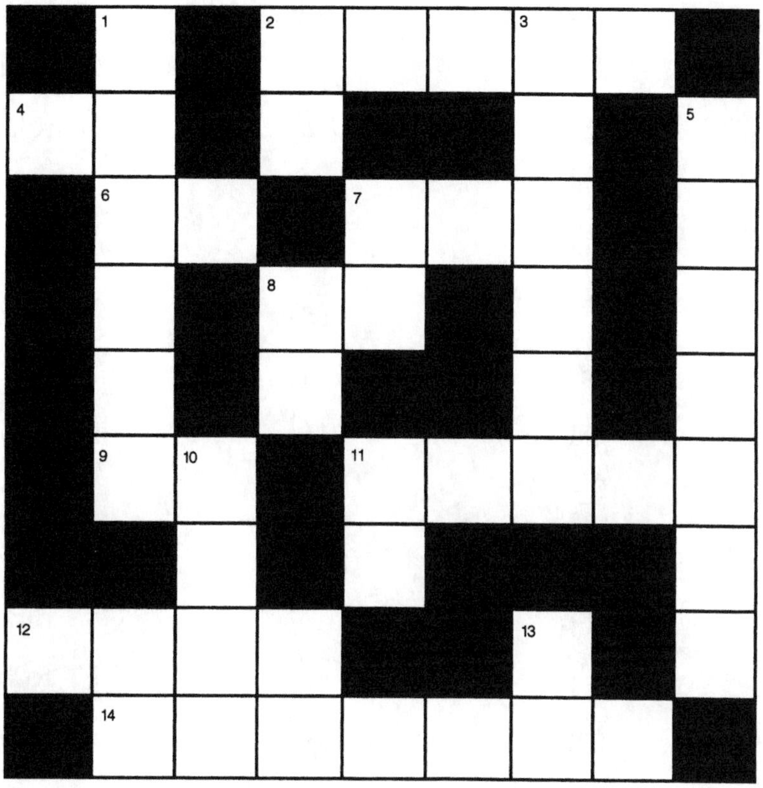

Across

2. America's nice, (but ...)
4. hometown
6. countryside
7. thinking of returning to one's (home) country
8. return home
9. mother
11. the four seasons are all nice
12. the scenery is very beautiful
14. Many people live in Beijing.

Down

1. return to one's hometown to see one's parents
2. US currency
3. what Beijing is (as stated by Wang Peng)
5. (it) truly is a nice place
7. to come back
10. a lot of relatives
11. 4 o'clock
13. northwest

II. Radical Identification.

Provide the Pīnyīn for each of the following characters and put the radical component each set has in common in the parentheses to the right.

路 ______	跑 ______	踢 ______	(______)
游 ______	泳 ______	淹 ______	(______)
胖 ______	腐 ______	腳 (脚) ______	(______)
廚 (厨) ______	樹 (树) ______	導 (导) ______	(______)

III. Matching.

First, draw a line connecting the Pīnyīn to its traditional character. Then, connect the traditional character to its simplified counterpart. Finally, draw a line connecting the simplified character to its English meaning.

Pīnyīn	Traditional	Simplified	English
ā	阿	镇	Prefix
bù	親	满	related by blood
chà	鄉	游	countryside
dǎo	鎮	雪	town
fēng	樹	部	tree
guā	滿	差	full
jì	風	树	wind
jiù	雪	济	snow
mǎn	迎	亲	to welcome
qīn	舊	迎	old
shù	濟	刮	to benefit
xiāng	部	阿	part
xuě	差	导	to blow
yíng	颳	旧	to guide
yóu	導	风	to travel
zhèn	遊	乡	to be short of

IV. Phonological Distinction.

Provide the **full** Pīnyīn for each of the following characters and then put the basic homonym (initial + final, but no tone) each set shares in the parentheses to the right.

寄 ______	季 ______	濟 (济) ______	(______)
真 ______	鎮 (镇) ______	針 (针) ______	(______)
瓜 ______	颳 (刮) ______	掛 (挂) ______	(______)
英 (英) ______	迎 (迎) ______	贏 (赢) ______	(______)
象 (象) ______	像 (像) ______	鄉 (乡) ______	(______)

Dialogue I

探		tàn (†) to visit	探	探 探				
		探						
探	扌	扩	抨	探				

拾		shí (†) to pick up	拾	拾 拾				
		拾						
拾	扌	拾						

醒		xǐng (†) to wake up	醒	醒 醒				
		醒						
醒	酉	醒						

停		tíng (598) to park; to stop	停	停 停				
		停						
停	亻	广	佇	倍	停			

托		tuō (†) to support w/ hands	托	托 托				
		托		託				
托	扌	扌	扦	托				

皮
pí (533)
skin; leather
皮 皮 皮
皮 𠂆 皮

箱
xiāng (†)
box; case; trunk
箱 箱 箱
箱 ⺮ 筣 箱

隨 随
suí (518)
to follow
隨 随 隨 隨 随 随
隨 阝 阝 陏 隋 隨
随 阝 阝 陏 随

稱 称
chēng (728)
to weigh
稱 称 稱 稱 称 称
稱 禾 禾 稍 稱 稱 稱
称 禾 称

超
chāo (†)
to exceed; to surpass
超 超 超
超 走 超

登		dēng (†) to board
登	癶	登

急		jí (500) urgent; pressing
急	𠂊	刍	急

哭		kū (738) to cry
哭	口	吅	哭

途	途	tú (†) road; way
途	人	余	途
途	人	余	途

順	顺	shùn (830) in the same direction
順	丿	川	川	順
顺	丿	川	川	顺

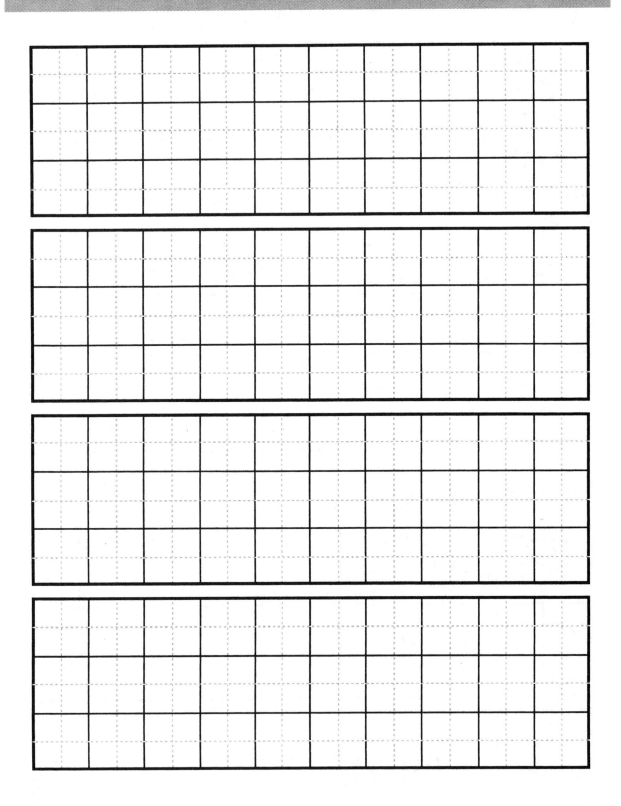

Dialogue II

		xīn (†)					
辛		suffering	辛	辛			
		辛					
辛	立	辛					

		kǔ (457)					
苦	苦	bitterness; pain	苦	苦			
		苦 苦		苦	苦		
苦	艹	苦					
苦	艹	苦					

		shòu (†)					
瘦		thin	瘦	瘦			
		瘦					
瘦	疒	瘦	瘦				

		jīn (847)					
斤		*jin* (Chn unit of weight)	斤	斤			
		斤					
斤	斤						

		lèi (†)					
累		to be tired	累	累			
		累					
累	田	累					

爺 爷

yé (387)

grandfather

爺 爷

爺 父

爷 父

奶 奶

nǎi (712)

breasts

奶 奶

奶 女

奶 女

孫 孙

sūn (†)

grandson

孫 孙

孫 子

孙 子 孙

爺 爺 爺

孫 孫 孫

Fun With Characters

I. Seek and Find.

Hidden in the box below are some words and phrases from the text. See how many you can find and circle them. Phrases can go horizontally left to right (→), vertically top to bottom (↓), or diagonally upper left to lower right (↘) or lower left to upper right (↗).

父	母	長	提	醒	表	多	小	前
位	親	戚	找	行	天	了	保	心
探	斤	五	號	門	李	北	超	重
放	辛	要	車	台	口	京	壞	人
暑	弟	汽	颱	風	送	首	飾	哥
假	租	多	順	我	們	都	高	興
出	不	路	停	飛	途	機	運	證
差	一	點	起	在	機	場	燈	登
過	身	累	座	公	隨	票	動	苦

II. Phonetic Identification.

Provide the Pīnyīn for each of the following characters and provide the "phonetic" ("sound radical/component") in the parentheses along with its Pīnyīn. The first one has been done for you.

除 (除)	chú	途 (途)	tú	(余	yú)
政	______	整	______	(______	______)
哥	______	河	______	(______	______)
拍	______	怕	______	(______	______)
新	______	近 (近)	______	(______	______)
機 (机)	______	磯 (矶)	______	(______	______)

III. MATCHING.

First, draw a line connecting the Pīnyīn to its traditional character. Then, connect the traditional character to its simplified counterpart. Finally, draw a line connecting the simplified character to its English meaning.

Pīnyīn	Traditional	Simplified	English
chēng	隨	奶	road
kǔ	稱	孙	breasts
nǎi	途	爷	to weigh
shùn	順	苦	to follow
suí	苦	顺	grandson
sūn	爺	途	bitterness
tú	奶	称	grandfather
yé	孫	随	in the same direction

IV. FILL IN THE SQUARES.

Fill in each of the empty squares below with one character each that contains the radical component provided.

	亻	

	扌	

	辶	

	女	

	日	

	頁	

	1	2	3	4	5	6	7	8	9	10	11	12
1												
2												
3												
4												
5												
6												
7												
8												
9												
10												
11												
12												
	1	2	3	4	5	6	7	8	9	10	11	12

	1	2	3	4	5	6	7	8	9	10	11	12
1												
2												
3												
4												
5												
6												
7												
8												
9												
10												
11												
12												
	1	2	3	4	5	6	7	8	9	10	11	12

INDEXES

Enlarged Characters for Easier Viewing

Lesson 13	Lesson 13	Lesson 13
職	驗	續
see page 13	*see page 15*	*see page 20*
zhí	yàn	xù

Lesson 14	Lesson 15	Lesson 15
離	禮	聰
see page 24	*see page 35*	*see page 35*
lí	lǐ	cōng

Lesson 15	Lesson 15	Lesson 15

see page 36	*see page 36*	*see page 38*
ài	shǔ	yīng

Lesson 16	Lesson 16	Lesson 16

see page 44	*see page 45*	*see page 47*
huài	yào	tǐ

Lesson 16	Lesson 17	Lesson 18

see page 48	*see page 55*	*see page 63*
yǎng	qìng	chú

Lesson 20	Lesson 20	Lesson 20

see page 80	*see page 85*	*see page 87*
lán	yā	yíng

Lesson 21	Lesson 21	Lesson 21
護	華	轉
see page 91	see page 94	see page 95
hù	huá	zhuǎn

Lesson 21	Lesson 22	Lesson 22
韓	舊	導
see page 96	see page 106	see page 108
hán	jiù	dǎo

Integrated Chinese I (Part 2) — Character Index
Chronological by Lesson

*	=	bound form
M	=	Measure word
P	=	Particle
QP	=	Question Particle

Lesson 12

務／务	wù	*service
桌	zhuō	table
菜／菜	cài	vegetable; dish
餃／饺	jiǎo	dumpling
素	sù	white; plain
盤／盘	pán	plate; dish
豆	dòu	bean
腐	fǔ	rotten; stale
肉	ròu	meat
碗	wǎn	bowl
酸	suān	sour
辣	là	spicy; hot
湯／汤	tāng	soup
放	fàng	put in; add
味	wèi	flavor
精	jīng	essence
渴	kě	thirsty
些	xiē	some
夠／够	gòu	enough
餓／饿	è	be hungry
傅	fù	teacher
糖	táng	sugar
醋	cù	vinegar
魚／鱼	yú	fish
甜	tián	sweet
極／极	jí	extreme
燒／烧	shāo	burn; cook
牛	niú	cow; ox
賣／卖	mài	sell
完	wán	finish
拌	bàn	mix
瓜	guā	melon
米	mǐ	rice

Lesson 13

借	jiè	borrow
帶／带	dài	belt; tape
職／职	zhí	duty; job
把	bǎ	Preposition
證／证	zhèng	evidence; certificate
留	liú	leave (behind); stay
言	yán	word
實／实	shí	reality; fact
驗／验	yàn	examine; check
樓／楼	lóu	floor; storey
還／还	huán	return
忘	wàng	forget
其	qí	he; she; it; they
卡	kǎ	block; check
關／关	guān	close
門／门	mén	door; gate
剩	shèng	remain; be left over
頭／头	tóu	head
及／及	jí	reach
本	běn	M (for books); origin
如	rú	like; as if
果	guǒ	fruit; result
罰／罚	fá	fine; punish
續／续	xù	continue; extend
必	bì	must
須／须	xū	must
典	diǎn	standard work

Lesson 14

運／运	yùn	carry; transport
動／动	dòng	move; stir
旁	páng	side
遠／远	yuǎn	far; distant

住	zhù	live
離／离	lí	from; away
活	huó	live
心	xīn	heart
店	diàn	store shop
田	tián	(a surname); field
金	jīn	(a surname); gold
城	chéng	city; town
閉／闭	bì	close
著／着	zhe	P
眼	yǎn	eye
睛	jīng	eyeball
從／从	cóng	from
直(直)	zhí	straight
往	wàng	towards
南	nán	south
口	kǒu	mouth
拐／拐	guǎi	turn
哎／哎	āi	Excl.
燈／灯	dēng	light; lamp
右	yòu	right
單／单	dān	one; single; odd
左	zuǒ	left
面	miàn	face; side
京	jīng	capital

Lesson 15

表	biǎo	outside; form
班	bān	class
汁	zhī	juice
接	jiē	meet; receive
林	lín	(a surname); forest
禮／礼	lǐ	gift
物	wù	thing; matter
聰／聪	cōng	acute hearing
暑	shǔ	heat; hot weather
長／长	zhǎng	grow; come into being
愛／爱	ài	love
屬／属	shǔ	belong to
狗	gǒu	dog
鼻	bí	nose
嘴	zuǐ	mouth
將／将	jiāng	going to
定	dìng	decide; fix; set
臉／脸	liǎn	face
腿／腿	tuǐ	leg
長／长	cháng	long
指	zhǐ	finger
應／应	yīng	should; ought to
該／该	gāi	should; ought to
彈／弹	tán	play
鋼／钢	gāng	steel
琴	qín	piano
倫／伦	lún	relationship
姆	mǔ	*nurse; *maid

Lesson 16

病	bìng	illness
肚	dù	stomach; belly
疼	téng	be painful
死	sǐ	die
廁／厕	cè	lavatory; toilet
躺	tǎng	lie down
檢／检	jiǎn	inspect; examine
查	chá	inspect; examine
壞／坏	huài	bad
針／针	zhēn	needle
種／种	zhǒng	kind; type
藥／药	yào	medicine
淚／泪	lèi	tear
流	liú	flow; shed
身	shēn	body
體／体	tǐ	body
癢／痒	yǎng	itch
敏	mǐn	quick; nimble

趕／赶	gǎn	hurry; rush
越	yuè	exceed; overstep
重	zhòng	serious; heavy
健／健	jiàn	healthy; strong
康	kāng	well-being; health
保	bǎo	protect
險／险	xiǎn	danger; risk
猜	cāi	guess
馬／马	mǎ	(a surname); horse

Lesson 17

參／参	cān	participate
加	jiā	add; put in
印	yìn	seal; stamp
象／象	xiàng	appearance
成	chéng	become; complete
演	yǎn	show; perform
費／费	fèi	spend; take (effort)
力	lì	power; strength
倆／俩	liǎ	M; two (people)
碼／码	mǎ	number
劇／剧	jù	play; opera
慶／庆	qìng	celebrate
掃／扫	sǎo	sweep
房／房	fáng	house; room
整	zhěng	neat; tidy
理	lǐ	tidy up; put in order
旅	lǚ	travel
係／系	xì	connection; tie
紐／纽	niǔ	button

Lesson 18

吵	chǎo	noisy
連／连	lián	even
準／准	zhǔn	acurate
備／备	bei	prepare
搬	bān	move
紙／纸	zhǐ	paper
／广	guǎng	broad; vast
附／附	fù	get close to
寓	yù	reside; live
里	lǐ	*li* (unit of length)
套	tào	suite/set
臥／卧	wò	lie (down)
廚／厨	chú	kitchen
傢／家	jiā	*furniture
俱／具	jù	all; complete
沙	shā	sand
椅	yǐ	chair
架	jià	frame; shelf
安	ān	peaceful; quiet
靜／静	jìng	quiet
非	fēi	not; no
元	yuán	*yuan* (currency)
押	yā	give as security
當／当	dāng	serve as; allow
許／许	xǔ	allow; be allowed
養／养	yǎng	raise

Lesson 19

郵／邮	yóu	mail; post
局	jú	office; bureau
寄	jì	mail; send by mail
營／营	yíng	operate; run
貼／贴	tiē	paste on; stick on
掛／挂	guà	hang
另	lìng	other
首	shǒu	head
飾／饰	shì	decorations
鮮／鲜	xiān	fresh
束	shù	M (for flowers, etc.)
訂／订	dìng	order; subscribe to
收	shōu	receive
存	cún	store; keep
支	zhī	pay out

它	tā	it
民	mín	people
幣／币	bì	currency
銀／银	yín	silver
行	háng	profession; firm

Lesson 20

胖	pàng	fat
怕	pà	fear; be afraid
簡／简	jiǎn	simple
跑	pǎo	run
受	shòu	bear; receive
網／网	wǎng	net
拍	pāi	racket; slap
籃／篮	lán	basket
游	yóu	swim; travel
泳	yǒng	swim
危	wēi	danger; peril
淹	yān	flood; submerge
願／愿	yuàn	be willing
調／调	tiáo	change to; adjust
足	zú	foot
賽／赛	sài	game; match
圓／圆	yuán	round
提	tí	carry; raise
際／际	jì	border; edge
式	shì	style; type
腳／脚	jiǎo	foot
踢	tī	kick
手	shǒu	hand
抱	bào	hold; hug
壓／压	yā	crush; press (down)
被	bèi	Preposition
擔／担	dān	carry (on a shoulder)
棒	bàng	strong; good
特	tè	special; particular
傷／伤	shāng	injure; hurt
輸／输	shū	lose (a game, etc.)
贏／赢	yíng	win (a game, etc.)

Lesson 21

計／计	jì	count; compute
劃／划	huà	plan; delimit
各	gè	each; every
護／护	hù	protect
簽／签	qiān	sign
航	háng	boat; ship; navigate
司	sī	manage; attend to
減／减	jiǎn	reduce; decrease
價／价	jià	price; value
社	shè	community; society
程	chéng	rule; order; journey
折	zhé	break; discount
頓／顿	dùn	M (for occurances)
華／华	huá	magnificent; China
初	chū	first; beginning
千	qiān	thousand
轉／转	zhuǎn	turn
內	nèi	inside
漲／涨	zhǎng	rise
盛	shèng	flourishing; abundant
韓／韩	hán	(a surname); Korea
芝／芝	zhī	*sesame (seed)
洛	luò	(name of a river)
杉	shān	China fir
磯／矶	jī	jetty
香	xiāng	fragrant
港	gǎng	port; harbor

Lesson 22

父	fù	father
母	mǔ	mother
婆	pó	old woman
阿／阿	ā	Prefix
姨	yí	aunt
親／亲	qīn	related by blood

戚	qī	relative
伯	bó	uncle
市	shì	city; market
鄉／乡	xiāng	countryside
啦	lā	P
鎮／镇	zhèn	town
座	zuò	M (for bridges, etc.)
山	shān	mountain
河	hé	river
樹／树	shù	tree
滿／满	mǎn	full
風／风	fēng	wind
景	jǐng	scenery; scene
季	jì	season
滑	huá	slide
雪／雪	xuě	snow
迎／迎	yíng	welcome
州	zhōu	state
舊／旧	jiù	old
較／较	jiào	compare
政	zhèng	politics
治	zhì	govern
濟／济	jì	help; benefit
部／部	bù	part; section
颳／刮	guā	blow
導／导	dǎo	lead; guide
遊／游	yóu	travel; tour

Lesson 23

探	tàn	visit
拾	shí	pick up
提	tí	carry; raise
醒	xǐng	wake up
差／差	chà	wanting; short of
停	tíng	park; stop
托(託)	tuō	ask; entrust
皮	pí	skin; leather
箱	xiāng	box; case; trunk
隨／随	suī	follow
拿	ná	take
稱／称	chēng	weigh
超	chāo	exceed; surpass
登	dēng	board
急	jí	urgent; pressing
哭	kū	cry
途／途	tú	road; way
順／顺	shùn	in the same direction
辛	xīn	suffering
苦／苦	kǔ	bitterness; pain
瘦	shòu	thin
斤	jīn	*jin* (unit of weight)
累	lèi	be tired
爺／爷	yé	grandfather
奶／奶	nǎi	breasts
孫／孙	kū	grandson

Integrated Chinese I (Parts 1 & 2) — Character Index
Alphabetical by Pīnyīn

*	=	bound form
M	=	Measure word
P	=	Particle
QP	=	Question Particle

A

阿／阿	ā	Prefix	22.1
啊／啊	a	P	6.2
哎／哎	āi	Excl.	14.2
愛／爱	ài	love	15.2
安	ān	peaceful; quiet	18

B

八	bā	eight	Num
把	bǎ	Preposition	13.1
爸	bà	dad	2.1
吧	ba	P	5.1
白	bái	white	3.1
百	bǎi	hundred	9.1
班	bān	class	15.1
搬	bān	move	18
半	bàn	half	3.1
辦／办	bàn	manage	6.1
拌	bàn	mix	12.2
幫／帮	bāng	help	6.2
棒	bàng	strong; good	20.2
保	bǎo	protect	16.2
報／报	bào	newspaper	8.1
抱	bào	hold; hug	20.2
杯	bēi	cup; glass	5.1
北	běi	north	10.2
備／备	bèi	prepare	18
被	bèi	Preposition	20.2
本	běn	M (for books)	13.2
鼻	bí	nose	15.2
筆／笔	bǐ	pen	7.1
比	bǐ	compare	10.1
必	bì	must	13.2
閉／闭	bì	close	14.2
幣／币	bì	currency	19.2
邊／边	biān	side	8.1
便	biàn	convenient	6.1
表	biǎo	outside; form	15.1
別／别	bié	other	4.2
病	bìng	illness	16.1
伯	bó	uncle	22.1
不	bù	not; no	1.2
步	bù	step	8.2
部／部	bù	part; section	22.2

C

猜	cāi	guess	16.2
才	cái	not until; only	5.2
菜／菜	cài	vegetable; dish	12.1
餐	cān	meal	8.1
參／参	cān	participate	17.1
廁／厕	cè	lavatory; toilet	16.1
茶／茶	chá	tea	5.1
查	chá	inspect; examine	16.1
差／差	chà	wanting; short of	23.1
常	cháng	often	4.1
長／长	cháng	long	15.2
場／场	chǎng	field	11.1
唱	chàng	sing	4.1
超	chāo	exceed; surpass	23.1
吵	chǎo	noisy	18
車／车	chē	car	11.1
襯／衬	chèn	lining	9.1
稱／称	chēng	weigh	23.1
成	chéng	complete	17.1
城	chéng	city; town	14.2
程	chéng	rule; order; journey	21.1
吃	chī	eat	3.1
出	chū	go out	10.2

初	chū	first; beginning	21.2
除／除	chú	except	8.2
廚／厨	chú	kitchen	18
楚	chǔ	clear; neat	8.2
穿	chuān	wear	9.1
床(牀)	chuáng	bed	8.1
春	chūn	spring	10.2
詞／词	cí	word	7.1
次	cì	M (for occurances)	10.2
聰／聪	cōng	acute hearing	15.2
從／从	cóng	from	14.2
醋	cù	vinegar	12.2
存	cún	store; keep	19.2
错／错	cuò	wrong; error	4.2

D

打	dǎ	hit; strike	4.1
大	dà	big	3.1
帶／带	dài	belt; tape	13.1
單／单	dān	one; single; odd	14.2
擔／担	dān	carry	20.2
但	dàn	but	6.2
當／当	dāng	serve as; allow	18
導／导	dǎo	lead; guide	22.2
到	dào	arrive	6.1
道／道	dào	road; way	6.2
得	dé	obtain; get	4.2
的	de	P	2.1
得	de	P	7.1
得	děi	must; have to	6.1
燈／灯	dēng	light; lamp	14.2
登	dēng	board	23.1
等	děng	wait	6.1
弟	dì	younger brother	2.1
第	dì	(ordinal prefix)	7.1
地	dì	earth	11.1
點／点	diǎn	dot; o'clock	3.1
典	diǎn	standard work	13.2
電／电	diàn	electric	4.1
店	diàn	store shop	14.1
定	dìng	decide; fix; set	15.2
訂／订	dìng	order; subscribe to	19.2
東／东	dōng	east	9.1
冬	dōng	winter	10.2
懂／懂	dǒng	understand	7.1
動／动	dòng	move; stir	14.1
都／都	dōu	all; both	2.2
豆	dòu	bean	12.1
都／都	dū	capital	22.2
肚	dù	stomach; belly	16.1
對／对	duì	correct; toward	4.1
頓／顿	dùn	M (for occurances)	21.1
多	duō	many	3.1

E

餓／饿	è	be hungry	12.1
兒／儿	ér	son; child	2.1
而	ér	and	10.1
二	èr	two	Num

F

發／发	fā	emit; issue	8.1
罰／罚	fá	fine; punish	13.2
法	fǎ	method; way	7.1
煩／烦	fán	bother	11.1
飯／饭	fàn	meal	3.1
方	fāng	square; side	6.1
房／房	fáng	house; room	17.2
放	fàng	put in; add	12.1
啡	fēi	*coffee	5.1
飛／飞	fēi	fly	11.1
非	fēi	not; no	18
費／费	fèi	spend; take (effort)	17.1
分	fēn	penny; minute	9.1
封	fēng	M (for letters)	8.2
風／风	fēng	wind	22.1

服	fú	clothing	9.1
腐	fǔ	rotten; stale	12.1
復／复	fù	duplicate	7.1
付	fù	pay	9.1
傅	fù	teacher	12.2
附／附	fù	get close to	18
父	fù	father	22.1

G

該／该	gāi	should; ought to	15.2
趕／赶	gǎn	hurry; rush	16.2
剛／刚	gāng	just now	10.2
鋼／钢	gāng	steel	15.2
港	gǎng	port; harbor	21.2
高	gāo	tall	2.1
糕	gāo	cake	10.2
告	gào	tell; inform	8.1
哥	gē	older brother	2.2
歌	gē	song	4.1
個／个	gè	M (general)	2.1
各	gè	each; every	21.1
給／给	gěi	give	5.1
跟	gēn	with	6.2
更	gèng	even more	10.1
工	gōng	craft; work	5.1
公	gōng	public	6.1
功	gōng	skill	7.2
共	gòng	altogether	9.1
狗	gǒu	dog	15.2
夠／够	gòu	enough	12.1
瓜	guā	melon	12.2
颳／刮	guā	blow	22.2
掛／挂	guà	hang	19.1
拐／拐	guǎi	turn	14.2
關／关	guān	close	13.1
館／馆	guǎn	accommodations	5.2
慣／惯	guàn	be used to	8.2
／广	guǎng	broad; vast	18
貴／贵	guì	honorable	1.1
國／国	guó	country	1.2
果	guǒ	fruit; result	13.2
過／过	guò	pass	11.2

H

孩	hái	child	2.1
還／还	hái	still; yet	3.1
海	hǎi	sea	10.1
寒	hán	cold	11.1
韓／韩	hán	(a surname); Korea	21.2
漢／汉	hàn	Chinese	7.1
行	háng	profession; firm	19.2
航	háng	boat; ship	21.1
好	hǎo	fine; good; OK	1.1
號／号	hào	number	3.1
喝	hē	drink	5.1
和	hé	and	2.2
合	hé	suit; agree	9.2
河	hé	river	22.1
黑	hēi	black	9.2
很	hěn	very	3.2
紅／红	hóng	red	9.1
後／后	hòu	after	6.1
護／护	hù	protect	21.1
花／花	huā	spend	11.2
華／华	huá	magnificent; China	21.1
滑	huá	slide	22.1
話／话	huà	speech	6.1
劃／划	huà	plan; delimit	21.1
化	huá	to change	22.2
壞／坏	huài	bad	16.1
歡／欢	huān	joyful	3.1
還／还	huán	return	13.1
換／换	huàn	change	9.2
黃(黄)	huáng	yellow	9.1

回	huí	return	5.2
會／会	huì	meet	6.1
活	huó	live	14.1
火	huǒ	fire	Rad
貨／货	huò	merchandise	9.1
或	huò	or	11.1

J

機／机	jī	machine	11.1
磯／矶	jī	a rock over water	21.2
級／级	jí	grade; level	6.1
極／极	jí	extreme	12.2
及	jí	reach	13.1
急	jí	urgent; pressing	23.1
幾／几	jǐ	QP; how many	2.2
己	jǐ	oneself	11.2
記／记	jì	record	8.1
寄	jì	mail; send by mail	19.1
際／际	jì	border; edge	20.2
計／计	jì	count; compute	21.1
季	jì	season	22.1
濟／济	jì	help; benefit	22.2
家	jiā	family; home	2.2
加	jiā	add; put in	17.1
傢／家	jiā	*furniture	18
假	jià	vacation	11.1
架	jià	frame; shelf	18
價／价	jià	price; value	21.1
間／间	jiān	M (for rooms)	6.1
檢／检	jiǎn	inspect; examine	16.1
簡／简	jiǎn	simple	20.1
減／减	jiǎn	reduce; decrease	21.1
見／见	jiàn	see	3.1
件	jiàn	M (for items)	9.1
健／健	jiàn	healthy; strong	16.2
將／将	jiāng	going to	15.2
教(教)	jiāo	teach	7.1
餃／饺	jiǎo	dumpling	12.1
腳／脚	jiǎo	foot	20.2
叫	jiào	call	1.1
覺／觉	jiào	feel; reckon	4.2
接	jiē	meet; receive	15.1
節／节	jié	M (for classes)	6.1
姐	jiě	older sister	1.1
介	jiè	between	5.1
借	jiè	borrow	13.1
今	jīn	today; now	3.1
金	jīn	(a surname); gold	14.1
斤	jīn	*jin* (unit of weight)	17.1
緊／紧	jǐn	tight	11.2
進／进	jìn	enter	5.1
近／近	jìn	near	8.2
經／经	jīng	pass through	8.1
精	jīng	essence	12.1
京	jīng	capital	14.2
睛	jīng	eyeball	14.2
景	jǐng	scenery; scene	22.1
靜／静	jìng	quiet	18
九	jiǔ	nine	Num
久	jiǔ	long time	4.2
酒	jiǔ	wine	5.1
就	jiù	just	6.1
舊／旧	jiù	old	22.1
局	jú	office; bureau	19.1
劇／剧	jù	play; opera	17.2
俱／具	jù	all; complete	18
覺／觉	jué	feel; reckon	4.2

K

咖	kā	*coffee	5.1
卡	kǎ	block; check	13.1
開／开	kāi	open	6.1
看	kàn	see; look	4.1
康	kāng	well-being; health	16.2

考	kǎo	test	6.1
可	kě	but	3.1
渴	kě	thirsty	12.1
刻	kè	quarter (hour)	3.2
客	kè	guest	4.1
課／课	kè	class; lesson	6.1
空	kòng	free time	6.1
口	kǒu	mouth	14.2
哭	kū	cry	23.1
苦／苦	kǔ	bitterness; pain	23.2
褲／裤	kù	pants	9.1
快	kuài	fast; quick	5.1
塊／块	kuài	piece; dollar	9.1

L

啦	lā	P	22.1
辣	là	spicy; hot	12.1
來／来	lái	come	5.1
藍／蓝	lán	blue	11.1
籃／篮	lán	basket	20.1
老	lǎo	old	1.2
樂／乐	lè	happy	5.1 (4.1)
了	le	P	3.1
淚／泪	lèi	tear	16.2
累	lèi	be tired	23.2
冷	lěng	cold	10.2
離／离	lí	from; away	14.1
李	lǐ	(a surname); plum	1.1
裏／里	lǐ	inside	7.1
禮／礼	lǐ	gift	15.2
理	lǐ	tidy up	17.2
里	lǐ	*li* (unit of length)	18
力	lì	power; strength	17.1
倆／俩	liǎ	M; two (people)	17.1
連／连	lián	even	18
臉／脸	liǎn	face	15.2
練／练	liàn	practice; drill	6.2
涼／凉	liáng	cool	10.2
兩／两	liǎng	two; a couple	2.2
亮／亮	liàng	bright	5.1
聊	liáo	chat	5.2
林	lín	(a surname); forest	15.1
另	lìng	other	19.1
留	liú	leave (behind)	13.1
流	liú	flow; shed	16.2
六	liù	six	Num
樓／楼	lóu	floor; storey	13.1
錄／录	lù	record	7.2
路	lù	road; way	11.2
旅	lǚ	travel	17.2
律	lǜ	law; rule	2.2
綠	lǜ	green	11.1
倫／伦	lún	relationship	15.2
洛	luò	(name of a river)	21.2

M

媽／妈	mā	mom	2.1
麻	má	hemp; numb	11.1
馬／马	mǎ	horse	16.2
碼／码	mǎ	number	17.2
嗎／吗	ma	QP	1.2
買／买	mǎi	buy	9.1
賣／卖	mài	sell	12.2
滿／满	mǎn	full	22.1
慢	màn	slow	7.1
忙	máng	busy	3.2
毛	máo	hair; dime	9.1
麼／么	me	*QP	1.1
没(沒)	méi	(have) not	2.1
美	měi	beautiful	1.2
每	měi	every; each	11.2
妹	mèi	younger sister	2.1
悶／闷	mēn	stuffy	10.2
門／门	mén	door; gate	13.1
們／们	men	*(plural suffix)	3.1

米	mǐ	rice	12.2
面	miàn	face; side	14.2
民	mín	people	19.2
敏	mǐn	quick; nimble	16.2
名	míng	name	1.1
明	míng	bright	3.2
末	mò	end	4.1
姆	mǔ	*nurse; *maid	15.2
母	mǔ	mother	22.1

N

拿	ná	take	16.2
哪／哪	nǎ / něi	which	5.1
那／那	nà / nèi	that	2.1
奶／奶	nǎi	breasts	23.2
男	nán	male	2.1
難／难	nán	difficult; hard	7.1
南	nán	south	14.2
腦／脑	nǎo	brain	8.1
呢	ne	QP	1.1
內	nèi	inside	21.2
能	néng	be able	8.2
你	nǐ	you	1.1
年	nián	year	3.1
唸／念	niàn	read	7.2
您	nín	you (polite)	1.1
牛	niú	cow; ox	12.2
紐／纽	niǔ	button	17.2
暖	nuǎn	warm	10.1
女	nǚ	woman; female	2.1

P

怕	pà	fear; be afraid	20.1
拍	pāi	racket; slap	20.1
盤／盘	pán	plate; dish	12.1
旁	páng	side	14.1
胖	pàng	fat	20.1
跑	pǎo	run	20.1
朋	péng	friend	1.1
啤	pí	*beer	5.1
皮	pí	skin; leather	23.1
篇	piān	M (for articles)	8.1
便	pián	*inexpensive	9.1
片	piàn	slice; *film	2.1
漂	piào	*pretty	5.1
票	piào	ticket	11.1
瓶	píng	bottle	5.2
平	píng	level; even	7.2
婆	pó	old woman	22.1

Q

七	qī	seven	Num
期	qī	period (of time)	3.1
戚	qī	relative	22.1
其	qí	he; she; it; they	13.1
起	qǐ	rise	5.1
氣／气	qì	air	6.1
汽	qì	steam	11.1
簽／签	qiān	sign	21.1
千	qiān	thousand	21.2
前	qián	front; before	8.1
錢／钱	qián	money	9.1
且	qiě	for the time being	10.1
親／亲	qīn	related by blood	22.1
琴	qín	piano	15.2
清	qīng	clear; clean	8.2
請／请	qǐng	please; invite	1.1
慶／庆	qìng	celebrate	17.2
秋	qiū	autumn; fall	10.2
球	qiú	ball	4.1
去	qù	go	4.1

R

然	rán	like that; so	9.2
讓／让	ràng	let; allow	11.2
熱／热	rè	hot	10.2

人	rén	man; person	1.2
認／认	rèn	to recognize	3.2
日	rì	sun; day	3.1
容	róng	hold; contain	7.1
肉	ròu	meat	12.1
如	rú	like; as if	13.2

S

賽／赛	sài	game; match	20.2
三	sān	three	Num
掃／扫	sǎo	sweep	17.2
色	sè	color	9.1
沙	shā	sand	18
衫	shān	shirt	9.1
杉	shān	China fir	21.2
山	shān	mountain	22.1
傷／伤	shāng	injure; hurt	20.2
上	shàng	above; on top	3.1
燒／烧	shāo	burn; cook	12.2
少	shǎo	few	9.1
紹／绍	shào	carry on	5.1
舍	shè	house	8.1
社	shè	community; society	21.1
誰／谁	shéi	who	2.1
身	shēn	body	16.2
什(甚)	shén	*what	1.1
生	shēng	be born	1.1
剩	shèng	remain	13.1
盛	shèng	flourishing	21.2
師／师	shī	teacher	1.2
十	shí	ten	Num
識／识	shí	to recognize	3.2
時／时	shí	time	4.1
實／实	shí	reality; fact	13.1
拾	shí	pick up	23.1
始	shǐ	begin	7.2
是	shì	be	1.2
事	shì	matter; affair	3.2
視／视	shì	view	4.1
室	shì	room	6.1
試／试	shì	try	6.1
適／适	shì	suit; fit	9.2
飾／饰	shì	decorations	19.2
式	shì	style; type	20.2
市	shì	city; market	22.1
收	shōu	receive	19.2
首	shǒu	head	19.2
手	shǒu	hand	20.2
售	shòu	sell	9.1
受	shòu	bear; receive	20.1
瘦	shòu	thin	23.2
書／书	shū	book	4.1
舒	shū	stretch	10.2
輸／输	shū	lose (a game, etc.)	20.2
屬／属	shǔ	belong to	15.2
暑	shǔ	heat; hot weather	15.2
束	shù	M (for flowers, etc.)	19.2
樹／树	shù	tree	22.1
帥	shuài	handsome	7.2
雙／双	shuāng	pair	9.2
水	shuǐ	water	5.1
睡	shuì	sleep	4.2
順／顺	shùn	in the same direction	23.1
說／说	shuō	speak	6.2
思	sī	think	4.2
司	sī	manage; attend to	21.1
死	sǐ	die	16.1
四	sì	four	Num
送／送	sòng	deliver	11.1
宿	sù	stay	8.1
訴／诉	sù	tell; relate	8.1
速／速	sù	speed	11.2
素	sù	white; plain	12.1
酸	suān	sour	12.1
算	suàn	calculate; figure	4.2

雖／虽	suī	though; while	9.2
隨／随	suí	follow	23.1
歲／岁	suì	age	3.1
孫／孙	sūn	grandson	23.2
所(所)	suǒ	*so; place	4.1

T

他	tā	he	2.1
她	tā	she	2.1
它	tā	it	19.2
台(臺)	tái	platform	10.2
太	tài	too; extremely	3.1
彈／弹	tán	play	15.2
探	tàn	visit	23.1
湯／汤	tāng	soup	12.1
糖	táng	sugar	12.2
躺	tǎng	lie down	16.1
套	tào	suite/set	18
特	tè	special; particular	20.2
疼	téng	be painful	16.1
踢	tī	kick	20.2
題／题	tí	topic; question	6.1
提	tí	carry; raise	20.2
體／体	tǐ	body	16.2
天	tiān	sky; day	3.1
田	tián	(a surname); field	14.1
甜	tián	sweet	12.2
條／条	tiáo	M (for long objects)	9.1
調／调	tiáo	change to; adjust	20.2
跳	tiào	jump	4.1
貼／贴	tiē	paste on; stick on	19.1
鐵／铁	tiě	iron	11.1
聽／听	tīng	listen	4.1
廳／厅	tīng	hall	8.1
停	tíng	park; stop	23.1
同	tóng	same	3.2
頭／头	tóu	head	13.1
圖／图	tú	drawing	5.2
途／途	tú	road; way	23.1
腿／腿	tuǐ	leg	15.2
托(託)	tuō	ask; entrust	23.1

W

外	wài	outside	4.1
灣／湾	wān	strait; bay	10.2
玩	wán	play; visit	5.2
完	wán	finish	12.2
晚／晚	wǎn	evening; late	3.1
碗	wǎn	bowl	12.1
王	wáng	(a surname); king	1.1
網／网	wǎng	net	20.1
望／望	wàng	hope; wish	8.2
忘	wàng	forget	13.1
往	wàng	towards	14.2
危	wēi	danger; peril	20.1
為／为	wèi	for	3.2
位	wèi	M (polite)	6.1
喂	wèi	Hello!; Hey!	6.1
味	wèi	flavor	12.1
文	wén	(written) language	2.2
問	wèn	ask	1.1
我	wǒ	I; me	1.1
臥／卧	wò	lie (down)	18
務／务	wù	*service	12.1
舞	wǔ	dance	4.1
物	wù	thing; matter	15.2

X

希	xī	hope	8.2
西	xī	west	9.1
習／习	xí	study; review	6.2
喜	xǐ	like; happy	3.1
洗	xǐ	wash	8.1
係／系	xì	connection; tie	17.2
下	xià	below; under	5.1
夏	xià	summer	10.2

先	xiān	first	1.1
鮮／鲜	xiān	fresh	19.2
險／险	xiǎn	danger; risk	16.2
現／现	xiàn	present	3.2
線／线	xiàn	line	11.1
香	xiāng	fragrant	21.2
鄉／乡	xiāng	countryside	22.1
箱	xiāng	box; case; trunk	23.1
想	xiǎng	think	4.2
像／像	xiàng	image	10.1
像／像	xiàng	to resemble	15.2
象／象	xiàng	appearance	17.1
小	xiǎo	little; small	1.1
校	xiào	school	5.1
笑	xiào	laugh	8.2
些	xiē	some	12.1
鞋	xié	shoes	9.2
寫／写	xiě	write	7.1
謝／谢	xiè	thank	3.1
新	xīn	new	8.1
心	xīn	heart	14.1
辛	xīn	suffering	23.2
信	xìn	letter	8.2
星	xīng	star	3.1
行	xíng	all right; O.K.	6.1
醒	xǐng	wake up	23.1
興	xìng	mood; interest	5.1
姓	xìng	surname	1.1
須／须	xū	must	13.2
許／许	xǔ	allow; be allowed	18.2
續／续	xù	continue; extend	13.2
學／学	xué	study	1.2
雪／雪	xuě	snow	22.1

Y

押	yā	pawn	18
壓／压	yā	crush; press (down)	20.2
呀	ya	P	5.1
淹	yān	flood; submerge	20.1
顏／颜	yán	face; countenance	9.1
言	yán	word	13.1
眼	yǎn	eye	14.2
演	yǎn	show; perform	17.1
驗／验	yàn	examine; check	13.1
癢／痒	yǎng	itch	16.2
養／养	yǎng	raise	18
樣／样	yàng	kind	3.1
要	yào	want	5.1
藥／药	yào	medicine	16.1
爺／爷	yé	grandfather	23.2
也	yě	also	1.2
夜	yè	night	7.2
業／业	yè	occupation	8.2
葉／叶	yè	leaf	10.1
一	yī	one	Num
醫／医	yī	doctor; medicine	2.2
衣	yī	clothing	9.1
宜	yí	suitable	9.1
姨	yí	aunt	22.1
以	yǐ	with	4.1
已	yǐ	already	8.1
椅	yǐ	chair	18
意	yì	meaning	4.2
易	yì	easy	7.1
因	yīn	because	3.2
音	yīn	sound; music	4.1
銀／银	yín	silver	19.2
印	yìn	seal; stamp	17.1
英／英	yīng	*England	2.2
應／应	yīng	should; ought to	15.2
迎／迎	yíng	welcome	22.1
營／营	yíng	operate; run	19.1
贏／赢	yíng	win (a game, etc.)	20.2
影	yǐng	shadow	4.1

泳	yǒng	swim	20.1
用	yòng	use	8.2
郵／邮	yóu	mail; post	19.1
游	yóu	swim; travel	20.1
遊／游	yóu	travel; tour	22.2
友	yǒu	friend	1.1
有	yǒu	have; there is/are	2.1
又	yòu	again	10.2
右	yòu	right	14.2
魚／鱼	yú	fish	12.2
寓	yù	reside; live	18
語／语	yǔ	language	7.1
雨	yǔ	rain	10.1
預／预	yù	prepare	7.1
員／员	yuán	personnel	9.1
園／园	yuán	garden	10.1
元	yuán	*yuan* (currency)	18
圓／圆	yuán	round	20.2
遠／远	yuǎn	far; distant	14.1
願／愿	yuàn	be willing	20.1
約／约	yuē	make an appoint.	10.1
月	yuè	moon; month	3.1
樂／乐	yuè	music	4.1
越	yuè	exceed; overstep	16.2
運／运	yùn	carry; transport	14.1

Z

再	zài	again	3.1
在	zài	at; in; on	3.2
糟	zāo	messy	10.2
早	zǎo	early	7.2
澡	zǎo	bath	8.1
怎	zěn	*how	3.1
站	zhàn	stand; station	11.1
張／张	zhāng	M; (a surname)	2.1
長／长	zhǎng	come into being	15.2
漲／涨	zhǎng	rise	21.2
找	zhǎo	look for; seek	4.2
照	zhào	shine	2.1
折	zhé	break; discount	21.1
者	zhě	(a suffix)	11.1
這／这	zhè(i)	this	2.1
著／着	zhe	P	14.2
真(眞)	zhēn	true; real	7.2
針／针	zhēn	needle	16.1
鎮／镇	zhèn	town	22.1
整	zhěng	neat; tidy	17.2
正	zhèng	just; straight	8.1
證／证	zhèng	evidence	13.1
政	zhèng	politics	22.2
知	zhī	know	6.2
汁	zhī	juice	15.1
支	zhī	pay out	19.2
芝／芝	zhī	*sesame (seed)	21.2
職／职	zhí	duty; job	13.1
直(直)	zhí	straight	14.2
只	zhǐ	only	4.2
指	zhǐ	finger	15.2
紙／纸	zhǐ	paper	18
治	zhì	govern	22.2
中	zhōng	center; middle	1.2
鐘／钟	zhōng	clock	3.1
種／种	zhǒng	kind; type	16.1
重	zhòng	serious; heavy	16.2
週／周	zhōu	week	4.1
州	zhōu	state	22.1
助	zhù	assist	7.1
祝	zhù	wish	8.2
住	zhù	live	14.1
專／专	zhuān	special	8.2
轉／转	zhuǎn	turn	21.2
準／准	zhǔn	accurate	18
桌	zhuō	table	12.1
子	zǐ	son	2.1

字	zì	character	1.1
自	zì	self	11.2
走	zǒu	walk	11.1
租	zū	rent	11.1
足	zú	foot	20.2
嘴	zuǐ	mouth	15.2
最	zuì	most	8.2
昨	zuó	yesterday	4.1
左	zuǒ	left	14.2
做	zuò	do	2.2
坐	zuò	sit	5.1
作	zuò	work; do	5.1
座	zuò	M (for bridges, etc.)	22.1

NOTES:

Integrated Chinese I (Parts 1 & 2)
Character Index — Traditional
Arranged by Number of Strokes

*	=	bound form
M	=	Measure word
P	=	Particle
QP	=	Question Particle

1

一	yī	one	Num

2

八	bā	eight	Num
二	èr	two	Num
九	jiǔ	nine	Num
了	le	P	3.1
力	lì	power; strength	17.1
七	qī	seven	Num
人	rén	man; person	1.2
十	shí	ten	Num
又	yòu	again	10.2

3

才	cái	not until; only	5.2
大	dà	big	3.1
工	gōng	craft; work	5.1
己	jǐ	oneself	11.2
久	jiǔ	long time	4.2
口	kǒu	mouth	23.2
女	nǚ	woman; female	2.1
千	qiān	thousand	21.2
三	sān	three	Num
山	shān	mountain	22.1
上	shàng	above; on top	3.1
下	xià	below; under	5.1
小	xiǎo	little; small	1.1
也	yě	also	1.2
已	yǐ	already	8.1
子	zǐ	son	2.1

4

比	bǐ	compare	10.1
不	bù	not; no	1.2
方	fāng	square; side	6.1
分	fēn	penny; minute	9.1
父	fù	father	22.1
公	gōng	public	6.1
化	huá	to change	22.2
及／及	jí	reach	13.1
介	jiè	between	5.1
今	jīn	today; now	3.1
斤	jīn	*jin* (unit of weight)	17.1
六	liù	six	Num
毛	máo	hair; dime	9.1
内	nèi	inside	21.2
牛	niú	cow; ox	12.2
片	piàn	slice; *film	2.1
日	rì	sun; day	3.1
少	shǎo	few	9.1
什	shén	*what	1.1
手	shǒu	hand	20.2
水	shuǐ	water	5.1
太	tài	too; extremely	3.1
天	tiān	sky; day	3.1
王	wáng	(a surname); king	1.1
文	wén	script	2.2
五	wǔ	five	Num
午	wǔ	noon	6.1
心	xīn	heart	14.1
以	yǐ	with	4.1
友	yǒu	friend	1.1
元	yuán	*yuan* (currency)	18.2
月	yuè	moon; month	3.1
支	zhī	pay out	19.2
中	zhōng	center; middle	1.2

5

白	bái	white	3.1
半	bàn	half	3.1
北	běi	north	10.2
本	běn	M (for books)	13.2
必	bì	must	13.2
出	chū	go out	10.2
打	dǎ	hit; strike	4.1
冬	dōng	winter	10.2
付	fù	pay	9.1
功	gōng	skill	7.2
瓜	guā	melon	12.2
加	jiā	add; put in	17.1
叫	jiào	call	1.1
卡	kǎ	block; check	13.1
可	kě	but	3.1
另	lìng	other	19.1
民	mín	people	19.2
末	mò	end	4.1
母	mǔ	mother	22.1
皮	pí	skin; leather	23.1
平	píng	level; even	7.2
且	qiě	for the time being	10.1
去	qù	go	4.1
生	shēng	be born	1.1
市	shì	city; market	22.1
司	sī	manage; attend to	21.1
四	sì	four	Num
他	tā	he	2.1
它	tā	it	19.2
台(臺)	tái	platform	10.2
田	tián	(a surname); field	14.1
外	wài	outside	4.1
印	yìn	seal; stamp	17.1
用	yòng	use	8.2
右	yòu	right	14.2
正	zhèng	just; straight	8.1
汁	zhī	juice	15.1
只	zhǐ	only	4.2
左	zuǒ	left	14.2

6

安	ān	peaceful; quiet	18.2
百	bǎi	hundred	9.1
吃	chī	eat	3.1
次	cì	M (for occurances)	10.2
存	cún	store; keep	19.2
地	dì	earth	11.1
多	duō	many	3.1
而	ér	and	10.1
各	gè	each; every	21.1
共	gòng	altogether	9.1
好	hǎo	fine; good; OK	1.1
合	hé	suit; agree	9.2
回	huí	return	5.2
件	jiàn	M (for items)	9.1
考	kǎo	test	6.1
老	lǎo	old	1.2
忙	máng	busy	3.2
米	mǐ	rice	12.2
名	míng	name	1.1
奶／奶	nǎi	breasts	23.2
年	nián	year	3.1
肉	ròu	meat	12.1
如	rú	like; as if	13.2
色	sè	color	9.1
式	shì	style; type	20.2
收	shōu	receive	19.2
死	sǐ	die	16.1
她	tā	she	2.1
同	tóng	same	3.2
托(託)	tuō	support (w/ hands)	23.1
危	wēi	danger; peril	20.1
西	xī	west	9.1
先	xiān	first	1.1

行	xíng	all right; O.K.	6.1
行	háng	profession; firm	19.2
衣	yī	clothing	9.1
因	yīn	because	3.2
有	yǒu	have; there is/are	2.1
再	zài	again	3.1
在	zài	at; in; on	3.2
早	zǎo	early	7.2
州	zhōu	state	22.1
字	zì	character	1.1
自	zì	self	11.2

7

把	bǎ	Preposition	13.1
吧	ba	P	5.1
別／别	bié	other	4.2
伯	bó	uncle	22.1
步	bù	step	8.2
吵	chǎo	noisy	18.1
車／车	chē	car	11.1
初	chū	first; beginning	21.2
床(牀)	chuáng	bed	8.1
但	dàn	but	6.2
弟	dì	younger brother	2.1
豆	dòu	bean	12.1
肚	dù	stomach; belly	16.1
告	gào	tell; inform	8.1
更	gèng	even more	10.1
見／见	jiàn	see	3.1
局	jú	office; bureau	19.1
快	kuài	fast; quick	5.1
冷	lěng	cold	10.2
李	lǐ	(a surname); plum	1.1
里	lǐ	*li* (unit of length)	18.1
没(沒)	méi	(have) not	2.1
每	měi	every; each	11.2
那／那	nà / nèi	that	2.1
男	nán	male	2.1
你	nǐ	you	1.1
汽	qì	steam	11.1
沙	shā	sand	18.2
杉	shān	China fir	21.2
社	shè	community; society	21.1
身	shēn	body	16.2
束	shù	M (for flowers, etc.)	19.2
辛	xīn	suffering	23.2
完	wán	finish	12.2
忘	wàng	forget	13.1
位	wèi	M (polite)	6.1
我	wǒ	I; me	1.1
希	xī	hope	8.2
言	yán	word	13.1
找	zhǎo	look for; seek	4.2
折	zhé	break; discount	21.1
芝／芝	zhī	*sesame (seed)	21.2
助	zhù	assist	7.1
住	zhù	live	14.1
走	zǒu	walk	11.1
足	zú	foot	20.2
坐	zuò	sit	5.1
作	zuò	work; do	5.1

8

阿／阿	ā	Prefix	22.1
爸	bà	dad	2.1
拌	bàn	mix	12.2
抱	bào	hold; hug	20.2
杯	bēi	cup; glass	5.1
表	biǎo	outside; form	15.1
長／长	cháng	long	15.2
到	dào	arrive	6.1
的	de	P	2.1
典	diǎn	standard work	13.2
店	diàn	store shop	14.1
定	dìng	decide; fix; set	15.2
東／东	dōng	east	9.1

兒／儿	ér	son; child	2.1
法	fǎ	method; way	7.1
房／房	fáng	house; room	17.2
放	fàng	put in; add	12.1
非	fēi	not; no	18.2
服	fú	clothing	9.1
附／附	fù	get close to	18.1
狗	gǒu	dog	15.2
拐／拐	guǎi	turn	14.2
果	guǒ	fruit; result	13.2
和	hé	and	2.2
河	hé	river	22.1
花／花	huā	spend	11.2
或	huò	or	11.1
季	jì	season	22.1
金	jīn	(a surname); gold	14.1
京	jīng	capital	14.2
刻	kè	quarter (hour)	3.2
來／来	lái	come	5.1
林	lín	(a surname); forest	15.1
門／门	mén	door; gate	13.1
姆	mǔ	*nurse; *maid	15.2
怕	pà	fear; be afraid	20.1
拍	pāi	racket; slap	20.1
其	qí	he; she; it; they	13.1
衫	shān	shirt	9.1
舍	shè	house	8.1
始	shǐ	begin	7.2
事	shì	matter; affair	3.2
受	shòu	bear; receive	20.1
所(所)	suǒ	*so; place	4.1
往	wàng	towards	14.2
味	wèi	flavor	12.1
臥／卧	wò	lie (down)	18.1
物	wù	thing; matter	15.2
些	xiē	some	12.1
姓	xìng	surname	1.1
押	yā	give as security	18.2
夜	yè	night	7.2
宜	yí	suitable	9.1
易	yì	easy	7.1
迎／迎	yíng	welcome	22.1
泳	yǒng	swim	20.1
雨	yǔ	rain	10.1
長／长	zhǎng	come into being	15.2
直(直)	zhí	straight	14.2
治	zhì	govern	22.2

9

哎／哎	āi	Excl.	14.2
保	bǎo	protect	16.2
便	biàn	convenient	6.1
查	chá	inspect; examine	16.1
城	chéng	city; town	14.2
穿	chuān	wear	9.1
春	chūn	spring	10.2
訂／订	dìng	order; subscribe to	19.2
飛／飞	fēi	fly	11.1
封	fēng	M (for letters)	8.2
風／风	fēng	wind	22.1
孩	hái	child	2.1
很	hěn	very	3.2
紅／红	hóng	red	9.1
候	hòu	wait	4.1
後／后	hòu	after	6.1
活	huó	live	14.1
計／计	jì	count; compute	21.1
架	jià	frame; shelf	18.2
看	kàn	see; look	4.1
客	kè	guest	4.1
苦／苦	kǔ	bitterness; pain	23.2
亮／亮	liàng	bright	5.1
律	lǜ	law; rule	2.2
洛	luò	(name of a river)	21.2

美	měi	beautiful	1.2
面	miàn	face; side	14.2
南	nán	south	14.2
胖	pàng	fat	20.1
便	pián	*inexpensive	9.1
前	qián	front; before	8.1
秋	qiū	autumn; fall	10.2
拾	shí	pick up	23.1
是	shì	be	1.2
室	shì	room	6.1
首	shǒu	head	19.2
帥	shuài	handsome	7.2
思	sī	think	4.2
為／为	wèi	for	3.2
洗	xǐ	wash	8.1
係／系	xì	connection; tie	17.2
香	xiāng	fragrant	21.2
信	xìn	letter	8.2
星	xīng	star	3.1
要	yào	want	5.1
姨	yí	aunt	22.1
音	yīn	sound; music	4.1
英／英	yīng	*England	2.2
約／约	yuē	make an appoint.	10.1
怎	zěn	*how	3.1
政	zhèng	politics	22.2
指	zhǐ	finger	15.2
重	zhòng	serious; heavy	16.2
祝	zhù	wish	8.2
昨	zuó	yesterday	4.1

10

班	bān	class	15.1
被	bèi	Preposition	20.2
病	bìng	illness	16.1
茶／茶	chá	tea	5.1
差／差	chà	wanting; short of	23.1
除／除	chú	except	8.2
剛／刚	gāng	just now	10.2
高	gāo	tall	2.1
哥	gē	older brother	2.2
個／个	gè	M (general)	2.1
國／国	guó	country	1.2
海	hǎi	sea	10.1
航	háng	boat; ship	21.1
級／级	jí	grade; level	6.1
記／记	jì	record	8.1
家	jiā	family; home	2.2
借	jiè	borrow	13.1
酒	jiǔ	wine	5.1
俱／具	jù	all; complete	18.1
哭	kū	cry	23.1
倆／俩	liǎ	M; two (people)	17.1
留	liú	leave (behind)	13.1
流	liú	flow; shed	16.2
旅	lǚ	travel	17.2
倫／伦	lún	relationship	15.2
馬／马	mǎ	horse	16.2
們／们	men	*(plural suffix)	3.1
拿	ná	take	16.2
哪／哪	nǎ / něi	which	5.1
能	néng	be able	8.2
紐／纽	niǔ	button	17.2
旁	páng	side	14.1
瓶	píng	bottle	5.2
起	qǐ	rise	5.1
氣／气	qì	air	6.1
容	róng	hold; contain	7.1
師／师	shī	teacher	1.2
時／时	shí	time	4.1
書／书	shū	book	4.1
送／送	sòng	deliver	11.1
素	sù	white; plain	12.1
孫／孙	sūn	grandson	23.2
套	tào	suite/set	18.1

特	tè	special; particular	20.2
疼	téng	be painful	16.1
夏	xià	summer	10.2
校	xiào	school	5.1
笑	xiào	laugh	8.2
員／员	yuán	personnel	9.1
站	zhàn	stand; station	11.1
真(眞)	zhēn	true; real	7.2
針／针	zhēn	needle	16.1
紙／纸	zhǐ	paper	18.1
桌	zhuō	table	12.1
租	zū	rent	11.1
座	zuò	M (for bridges, etc.)	22.1

11

啊／啊	a	P	6.2
閉／闭	bì	close	14.2
部／部	bù	part; section	22.2
猜	cāi	guess	16.2
參／参	cān	participate	17.1
常	cháng	often	4.1
唱	chàng	sing	4.1
從／从	cóng	from	14.2
帶／带	dài	belt; tape	13.1
得	dé	obtain; get	4.2
得	de	P	7.1
得	děi	must; have to	6.1 (4.2)
第	dì	(ordinal prefix)	7.1
動／动	dòng	move; stir	14.1
都／都	dōu	all; both	2.2
都／都	dū	capital	22.2
啡	fēi	*coffee	5.1
夠／够	gòu	enough	12.1
掛／挂	guà	hang	19.1
黃(黄)	huáng	yellow	9.1
貨／货	huò	merchandise	9.1
寄	jì	mail; send by mail	19.1
假	jià	vacation	11.1
健／健	jiàn	healthy; strong	16.2
將／将	jiāng	going to	15.2
教(敎)	jiāo	teach	7.1
接	jiē	meet; receive	15.1
康	kāng	well-being; health	16.2
啦	lā	P	22.1
淚／泪	lèi	tear	16.2
累	lèi	be tired	23.2
理	lǐ	tidy up	17.2
連／连	lián	even	18.1
涼／凉	liáng	cool	10.2
聊	liáo	chat	5.2
麻	má	hemp; numb	11.1
敏	mǐn	quick; nimble	16.2
唸／念	niàn	read	7.2
您	nín	you (polite)	1.1
啤	pí	*beer	5.1
票	piào	ticket	11.1
婆	pó	old woman	22.1
戚	qī	relative	22.1
清	qīng	clear; clean	8.2
球	qiú	ball	4.1
掃／扫	sǎo	sweep	17.2
紹／绍	shào	carry on	5.1
盛	shèng	flourishing	21.2
視／视	shì	view	4.1
售	shòu	sell	9.1
宿	sù	stay	8.1
速／速	sù	speed	11.2
探	tàn	visit	23.1
甜	tián	sweet	12.2
條／条	tiáo	M (for long objects)	9.1
停	tíng	park; stop	23.1
途／途	tú	road; way	23.1
望／望	wàng	hope; wish	8.2
問／问	wèn	ask	1.1

務／务	wù	*service	12.1
習／习	xí	study; review	6.2
現／现	xiàn	present	3.2
許／许	xú	allow; be allowed	18.2
雪／雪	xuě	snow	22.1
淹	yān	flood; submerge	20.1
眼	yǎn	eye	14.2
郵／邮	yóu	mail; post	19.1
魚／鱼	yú	fish	12.2
張／张	zhāng	M; (a surname)	2.1
這／这	zhè(i)	this	2.1
專／专	zhuān	special	8.2
做	zuò	do	2.2

12

棒	bàng	strong; good	20.2
報／报	bào	newspaper	8.1
備／备	bèi	prepare	18.1
筆／笔	bǐ	pen	7.1
菜／菜	cài	vegetable; dish	12.1
廁／厕	cè	lavatory; toilet	16.1
場／场	chǎng	field	11.1
超	chāo	exceed; surpass	23.1
程	chéng	rule; order; journey	21.1
詞／词	cí	word	7.1
單／单	dān	one; single; odd	14.2
登	dēng	board	23.1
等	děng	wait	6.1
發／发	fā	emit; issue	8.1
飯／饭	fàn	meal	3.1
費／费	fèi	spend; take (effort)	17.1
復／复	fù	duplicate	7.1
傅	fù	teacher	12.2
港	gǎng	port; harbor	21.2
給／给	gěi	give	5.1
貴／贵	guì	honorable	1.1
喝	hē	drink	5.1
黑	hēi	black	9.2
華／华	huá	magnificent; China	21.1
換／换	huàn	change	9.2
極／极	jí	extreme	12.2
幾／几	jǐ	QP; how many	2.2
傢／家	jiā	*furniture	18.1
間／间	jiān	M (for rooms)	6.1
減／减	jiǎn	reduce; decrease	21.1
進／进	jìn	enter	5.1
景	jǐng	scenery; scene	22.1
就	jiù	just	6.1
開／开	kāi	open	6.1
渴	kě	thirsty	12.1
裡 | 裏 | 里	lǐ	inside	7.1
買／买	mǎi	buy	9.1
悶／闷	mēn	stuffy	10.2
跑	pǎo	run	20.1
期	qī	period (of time)	3.1
琴	qín	piano	15.2
然	rán	like that; so	9.2
試／试	shì	try	6.1
剩	shèng	remain	13.1
舒	shū	stretch	10.2
暑	shǔ	heat; hot weather	15.2
順／顺	shùn	the same direction	23.1
訴／诉	sù	tell; relate	8.1
湯／汤	tāng	soup	12.1
提	tí	carry; raise	14.2
貼／贴	tiē	paste on; stick on	19.1
晚	wǎn	evening; late	3.1
喂	wéi/wèi	Hello!; Hey!	6.1
喜	xǐ	like; happy	3.1
鄉／乡	xiāng	countryside	22.1
象／象	xiàng	appearance	17.1
須／须	xū	must	13.2
葉／叶	yè	leaf	10.1
椅	yǐ	chair	18.2

游	yóu	swim; travel	20.1
寓	yù	reside; live	18.1
園／园	yuán	garden	10.1
越	yuè	exceed; overstep	16.2
著／着	zhe	P	14.2
週／周	zhōu	week	4.1
最	zuì	most	8.2

13

愛／爱	ài	love	15.2
搬	bān	move	18.1
楚	chǔ	clear; neat	8.2
當／当	dāng	serve as; allow	18.2
道／道	dào	road; way	6.2
電／电	diàn	electric	4.1
頓／顿	dùn	M (for occurances)	21.1
煩／烦	fán	bother	11.1
該／该	gāi	should; ought to	15.2
跟	gēn	with	6.2
過／过	guò	pass	11.2
號／号	hào	number	3.1
滑	huá	slide	22.1
話／话	huà	speech	6.1
會／会	huì	meet	6.1
腳／脚	jiǎo	foot	20.2
節／节	jié	M (for classes)	6.1
經／经	jīng	pass through	8.1
睛	jīng	eyeball	14.2
塊／块	kuài	piece; dollar	9.1
裏 | 裡 | 里	lǐ	inside	7.1
路	lù	road; way	11.2
媽／妈	mā	mom	2.1
嗎／吗	ma	QP	1.2
腦／脑	nǎo	brain	8.1
暖	nuǎn	warm	10.1
認／认	rèn	to recognize	3.2
傷／伤	shāng	injure; hurt	20.2
飾／饰	shì	decorations	19.2
睡	shuì	sleep	4.2
歲／岁	suì	age	3.1
跳	tiào	jump	4.1
碗	wǎn	bowl	12.1
想	xiǎng	think	4.2
新	xīn	new	8.1
爺／爷	yé	grandfather	23.2
業／业	yè	occupation	8.2
意	yì	meaning	4.2
遊／游	yóu	travel; tour	22.2
預／预	yù	prepare	7.1
圓／圆	yuán	round	20.2
運／运	yùn	carry; transport	14.1
照	zhào	shine	2.1
準／准	zhǔn	accurate	18.2

14

鼻	bí	nose	15.2
稱／称	chēng	weigh	23.1
對／对	duì	correct; toward	4.1
罰／罚	fá	fine; punish	13.2
腐	fǔ	rotten; stale	12.1
趕／赶	gǎn	hurry; rush	16.2
歌	gē	song	4.1
慣／惯	guàn	be used to	8.2
廣／广	guǎng	broad; vast	18.1
漢／汉	hàn	Chinese	7.1
劃／划	huà	plan; delimit	21.1
際／际	jì	border; edge	20.2
餃／饺	jiǎo	dumpling	12.1
精	jīng	essence	12.1
辣	là	spicy; hot	12.1
練／练	liàn	practice; drill	6.2
綠／绿	lǜ	green	11.1
滿／满	mǎn	full	22.1
慢	màn	slow	7.1

麼／么	me	*QP	1.1
漂	piào	*pretty	5.1
認／认	rèn	to recognize	3.2
實／实	shí	reality; fact	13.1
瘦	shòu	thin	23.2
說／说	shuō	speak	6.2
酸	suān	sour	12.1
算	suàn	calculate; figure	4.2
圖／图	tú	drawing	5.2
腿／腿	tuǐ	leg	15.2
網／网	wǎng	net	20.1
舞	wǔ	dance	4.1
像／像	xiàng	image	10.1
學／学	xué	study	1.2
演	yǎn	show; perform	17.1
銀／银	yín	silver	19.2
語／语	yǔ	language	7.1
遠／远	yuǎn	far; distant	14.1
漲／涨	zhǎng	rise	21.2
種／种	zhǒng	kind; type	16.1

15

幣／币	bì	currency	19.2
廚／厨	chú	kitchen	18.1
醋	cù	vinegar	12.2
餓／饿	è	be hungry	12.1
颳／刮	guā	blow	22.2
價／价	jià	price; value	21.1
劇／剧	jù	play; opera	17.2
課／课	kè	class; lesson	6.1
褲／裤	kù	pants	9.1
樂／乐	lè	happy	5.1 (4.1)
樓／楼	lóu	floor; storey	13.1
碼／码	mǎ	number	17.2
賣／卖	mài	sell	12.2
盤／盘	pán	plate; dish	12.1
篇	piān	M (for articles)	8.1
請／请	qǐng	please; invite	1.1
慶／庆	qìng	celebrate	17.2
熱／热	rè	hot	10.2
誰／谁	shéi	who	2.1
適／适	shì	suit; fit	9.2
彈／弹	tán	play	15.2
躺	tǎng	lie down	16.1
踢	tī	kick	20.2
調／调	tiáo	change to; adjust	20.2
線／线	xiàn	line	11.1
箱	xiāng	box; case; trunk	23.1
鞋	xié	shoes	9.2
養／养	yǎng	raise	18.2
樣／样	yàng	kind	3.1
影	yǐng	shadow	4.1
樂／乐	yuè	music	4.1

16

辦／办	bàn	manage	6.1
餐	cān	meal	8.1
錯／错	cuò	wrong; error	4.2
擔／担	dān	carry	20.2
導／导	dǎo	lead; guide	22.2
燈／灯	dēng	light; lamp	14.2
點／点	diǎn	dot; o'clock	3.1
懂／懂	dǒng	understand	7.1
鋼／钢	gāng	steel	15.2
糕	gāo	cake	10.2
館／馆	guǎn	accommodations	5.2
機／机	jī	machine	11.1
緊／紧	jǐn	tight	11.2
靜／静	jìng	quiet	18.2
錄／录	lù	record	7.2
錢／钱	qián	money	9.1
親／亲	qīn	related by blood	22.1
燒／烧	shāo	burn; cook	12.2
輸／输	shū	lose (a game, etc.)	20.2

樹／树	shù	tree	22.1
隨／随	suí	follow	23.1
糖	táng	sugar	12.2
頭／头	tóu	head	13.1
險／险	xiǎn	danger; risk	16.2
寫／写	xiě	write	7.1
醒	xǐng	wake up	23.1
興／兴	xìng	mood; interest	5.1
澡	zǎo	bath	8.1
整	zhěng	neat; tidy	17.2
嘴	zuǐ	mouth	15.2

17

幫／帮	bāng	help	6.2
聰／聪	cōng	acute hearing	15.2
還／还	hái	still; yet	3.1
韓／韩	hán	(a surname); Korea	21.2
還／还	huán	return	13.1
磯／矶	jī	a rock over water	21.2
濟／济	jì	help; benefit	22.2
檢／检	jiǎn	inspect; examine	16.1
禮／礼	lǐ	gift	15.2
臉／脸	liǎn	face	15.2
賽／赛	sài	game; match	20.2
雖／虽	suī	though; while	9.2
鮮／鲜	xiān	fresh	19.2
謝／谢	xiè	thank	3.1
壓／压	yā	crush; press (down)	20.2
應／应	yīng	should; ought to	15.2
營／营	yíng	operate; run	19.1
糟	zāo	messy	10.2

18

簡／简	jiǎn	simple	20.1
舊／旧	jiù	old	22.1
離／离	lí	from; away	14.1
雙／双	shuāng	pair	9.2
題／题	tí	topic; question	6.1
顏／颜	yán	face; countenance	9.1
醫／医	yī	doctor; medicine	2.2
鎮／镇	zhèn	town	22.1
職／职	zhí	duty; job	13.1
轉／转	zhuǎn	turn	21.2

19

邊／边	biān	side	8.1
關／关	guān	close	13.1
壞／坏	huài	bad	16.1
藍／蓝	lán	blue	11.1
難／难	nán	difficult; hard	7.1
簽／签	qiān	sign	21.1
識／识	shí	recognize	3.2
藥／药	yào	medicine	16.1
願／愿	yuàn	be willing	20.1
證／证	zhèng	evidence	13.1

20

籃／篮	lán	basket	20.1
癢／痒	yǎng	itch	16.2
贏／赢	yíng	win (a game, etc.)	20.2
鐘／钟	zhōng	clock	3.1

21

襯／衬	chèn	lining	9.1
覺／觉	jiào	feel; reckon	4.2
覺／觉	jué	feel; reckon	4.2
護／护	hù	protect	21.1
屬／属	shǔ	belong to	15.2
鐵／铁	tiě	iron	11.1
續／续	xù	continue; extend	13.2

22

歡／欢	huān	joyful	3.1
聽／听	tīng	listen	4.1

23

體／体	tǐ	body	16.2
驗／验	yàn	examine; check	13.1

24

讓／让	ràng	let; allow	11.2

25

廳／厅	tīng	hall	8.1
灣／湾	wān	strait; bay	10.2

NOTES:

Integrated Chinese I (Parts 1 & 2)
Character Index — Simplified
Arranged by Number of Strokes

*	=	bound form
M	=	Measure word
P	=	Particle
QP	=	Question Particle

1

一	yī	one	Num

2

八	bā	eight	Num
儿／兒	ér	son; child	2.1
二	èr	two	Num
几／幾	jǐ	QP; how many	2.2
九	jiǔ	nine	Num
了	le	P	3.1
力	lì	power; strength	17.1
七	qī	seven	Num
人	rén	man; person	1.2
十	shí	ten	Num
又	yòu	again	10.2

3

才	cái	not until; only	5.2
大	dà	big	3.1
飞／飛	fēi	fly	11.1
个／個	gè	M (general)	2.1
工	gōng	craft; work	5.1
广／廣	guǎng	broad; vast	18.1
及／及	jí	reach	13.1
己	jǐ	oneself	11.2
久	jiǔ	long time	4.2
口	kǒu	mouth	23.2
马／馬	mǎ	horse	16.2
么／麼	me	*QP	1.1
门／門	mén	door; gate	13.1
女	nǚ	woman; female	2.1
千	qiān	thousand	21.2
三	sān	three	Num
山	shān	mountain	22.1
上	shàng	above; on top	3.1
习／習	xí	study; review	6.2
下	xià	below; under	5.1
乡／鄉	xiāng	countryside	22.1
小	xiǎo	little; small	1.1
也	yě	also	1.2
已	yǐ	already	8.1
子	zǐ	son	2.1

4

办／辦	bàn	manage	6.1
比	bǐ	compare	10.1
币／幣	bì	currency	19.2
不	bù	not; no	1.2
长／長	cháng	long	15.2
车／車	chē	car	11.1
从／從	cóng	from	14.2
订／訂	dìng	order; subscribe to	19.2
方	fāng	square; side	6.1
分	fēn	penny; minute	9.1
风／風	fēng	wind	22.1
父	fù	father	22.1
公	gōng	public	6.1
化	huá	to change	22.2
计／計	jì	count; compute	21.1
见／見	jiàn	see	3.1
介	jiè	between	5.1
今	jīn	today; now	3.1
斤	jīn	*jin* (unit of weight)	17.1
开／開	kāi	open	6.1
六	liù	six	Num
毛	máo	hair; dime	9.1
内	nèi	inside	21.2
牛	niú	cow; ox	12.2

片	piàn	slice; *film	2.1
气／氣	qì	air	6.1
认／認	rèn	to recognize	3.2
日	rì	sun; day	3.1
少	shǎo	few	9.1
什	shén	*what	1.1
手	shǒu	hand	20.2
书／書	shū	book	4.1
双／雙	shuāng	pair	9.2
水	shuǐ	water	5.1
太	tài	too; extremely	3.1
天	tiān	sky; day	3.1
厅／廳	tīng	hall	8.1
王	wáng	(a surname); king	1.1
为／為	wèi	for	3.2
文	wén	script	2.2
五	wǔ	five	Num
午	wǔ	noon	6.1
心	xīn	heart	14.1
以	yǐ	with	4.1
友	yǒu	friend	1.1
元	yuán	*yuan* (currency)	18.2
月	yuè	moon; month	3.1
长／長	zhǎng	come into being	15.2
支	zhī	pay out	19.2
中	zhōng	center; middle	1.2
专／專	zhuān	special	8.2

5

白	bái	white	3.1
半	bàn	half	3.1
北	běi	north	10.2
本	běn	M (for books)	13.2
必	bì	must	13.2
边／邊	biān	side	8.1
出	chū	go out	10.2
打	dǎ	hit; strike	4.1
电／電	diàn	electric	4.1
东／東	dōng	east	9.1
冬	dōng	winter	10.2
对／對	duì	correct; toward	4.1
发／發	fā	emit; issue	8.1
付	fù	pay	9.1
功	gōng	skill	7.2
瓜	guā	melon	12.2
汉／漢	hàn	Chinese	7.1
号／號	hào	number	3.1
记／記	jì	record	8.1
加	jiā	add; put in	17.1
叫	jiào	call	1.1
节／節	jié	M (for classes)	6.1
旧／舊	jiù	old	22.1
卡	kǎ	block; check	13.1
可	kě	but	3.1
乐／樂	lè	happy	5.1 (4.1)
礼／禮	lǐ	gift	15.2
另	lìng	other	19.1
们／們	men	*(plural suffix)	3.1
民	mín	people	19.2
末	mò	end	4.1
母	mǔ	mother	22.1
奶／奶	nǎi	breasts	23.2
皮	pí	skin; leather	23.1
平	píng	level; even	7.2
且	qiě	for the time being	10.1
去	qù	go	4.1
让／讓	ràng	let; allow	11.2
生	shēng	be born	1.1
市	shì	city; market	22.1
司	sī	manage; attend to	21.1
四	sì	four	Num
帅／帥	shuài	handsome	7.2
他	tā	he	2.1
它	tā	it	19.2
台(臺)	tái	platform	10.2

田	tián	(a surname); field	14.1
头／頭	tóu	head	13.1
外	wài	outside	4.1
务／務	wù	*service	12.1
写／寫	xiě	write	7.1
业／業	yè	occupation	8.2
叶／葉	yè	leaf	10.1
印	yìn	seal; stamp	17.1
用	yòng	use	8.2
右	yòu	right	14.2
乐／樂	yuè	music	4.1
正	zhèng	just; straight	8.1
汁	zhī	juice	15.1
只	zhǐ	only	4.2
左	zuǒ	left	14.2

6

安	ān	peaceful; quiet	18.2
百	bǎi	hundred	9.1
闭／閉	bì	close	14.2
场／場	chǎng	field	11.1
吃	chī	eat	3.1
次	cì	M (for occurances)	10.2
存	cún	store; keep	19.2
当／當	dāng	serve as; allow	18.2
导／導	dǎo	lead; guide	22.2
灯／燈	dēng	light; lamp	14.2
地	dì	earth	11.1
动／動	dòng	move; stir	14.1
多	duō	many	3.1
而	ér	and	10.1
刚／剛	gāng	just now	10.2
各	gè	each; every	21.1
共	gòng	altogether	9.1
关／關	guān	close	13.1
过／過	guò	pass	11.2
行	háng	profession; firm	19.2
好	hǎo	fine; good; OK	1.1
合	hé	suit; agree	9.2
红／紅	hóng	red	9.1
后／後	hòu	after	6.1
华／華	huá	magnificent; China	21.1
划／劃	huà	plan; delimit	21.1
欢／歡	huān	joyful	3.1
回	huí	return	5.2
会／會	huì	meet	6.1
机／機	jī	machine	11.1
级／級	jí	grade; level	6.1
价／價	jià	price; value	21.1
件	jiàn	M (for items)	9.1
考	kǎo	test	6.1
老	lǎo	old	1.2
伦／倫	lún	relationship	15.2
媽／妈	mā	mom	2.1
嗎／吗	ma	QP	1.2
买／買	mǎi	buy	9.1
忙	máng	busy	3.2
米	mǐ	rice	12.2
名	míng	name	1.1
那／那	nà / nèi	that	2.1
年	nián	year	3.1
庆／慶	qìng	celebrate	17.2
肉	ròu	meat	12.1
如	rú	like; as if	13.2
扫／掃	sǎo	sweep	17.2
色	sè	color	9.1
伤／傷	shāng	injure; hurt	20.2
师／師	shī	teacher	1.2
式	shì	style; type	20.2
收	shōu	receive	19.2
死	sǐ	die	16.1
岁／歲	suì	age	3.1
孙／孫	sūn	grandson	23.2
她	tā	she	2.1

汤／湯	tāng	soup	12.1
同	tóng	same	3.2
托(託)	tuō	support (w/ hands)	23.1
网／網	wǎng	net	20.1
危	wēi	danger; peril	20.1
问／問	wèn	ask	1.1
西	xī	west	9.1
先	xiān	first	1.1
行	xíng	all right; O.K.	6.1
兴／興	xìng	mood; interest	5.1
许／許	xú	allow; be allowed	18.2
压／壓	yā	crush; press (down)	20.2
爷／爺	yé	grandfather	23.2
衣	yī	clothing	9.1
因	yīn	because	3.2
有	yǒu	have; there is/are	2.1
约／約	yuē	make an appoint.	10.1
再	zài	again	3.1
在	zài	at; in; on	3.2
早	zǎo	early	7.2
芝／芝	zhī	*sesame (seed)	21.2
州	zhōu	state	22.1
字	zì	character	1.1
自	zì	self	11.2

7

阿／阿	ā	Prefix	22.1
把	bǎ	Preposition	13.1
吧	ba	P	5.1
报／報	bào	newspaper	8.1
别／別	bié	other	4.2
伯	bó	uncle	22.1
步	bù	step	8.2
吵	chǎo	noisy	18.1
初	chū	first; beginning	21.2
床(牀)	chuáng	bed	8.1
词／詞	cí	word	7.1
但	dàn	but	6.2
弟	dì	younger brother	2.1
豆	dòu	bean	12.1
肚	dù	stomach; belly	16.1
饭／飯	fàn	meal	3.1
附／附	fù	get close to	18.1
告	gào	tell; inform	8.1
更	gèng	even more	10.1
还／還	hái	still; yet	3.1
护／護	hù	protect	21.1
花／花	huā	spend	11.2
坏／壞	huài	bad	16.1
还／還	huán	return	13.1
矶／磯	jī	a rock over water	21.2
极／極	jí	extreme	12.2
际／際	jì	border; edge	20.2
间／間	jiān	M (for rooms)	6.1
进／進	jìn	enter	5.1
局	jú	office; bureau	19.1
快	kuài	fast; quick	5.1
块／塊	kuài	piece; dollar	9.1
来／來	lái	come	5.1
冷	lěng	cold	10.2
李	lǐ	(a surname); plum	1.1
里 | 裡 | 裏	lǐ	inside	7.1
里	lǐ	*li* (unit of length)	18.1
连／連	lián	even	18.1
两／兩	liǎng	two; a couple	2.2
没(沒)	méi	(have) not	2.1
每	měi	every; each	11.2
闷／悶	mēn	stuffy	10.2
男	nán	male	2.1
你	nǐ	you	1.1
纽／紐	niǔ	button	17.2
汽	qì	steam	11.1
沙	shā	sand	18.2
杉	shān	China fir	21.2
社	shè	community; society	21.1

身	shēn	body	16.2
时／時	shí	time	4.1
识／識	shí	recognize	3.2
束	shù	M (for flowers, etc.)	19.2
诉／訴	sù	tell; relate	8.1
体／體	tǐ	body	16.2
条／條	tiáo	M (for long objects)	9.1
听／聽	tīng	listen	4.1
系／係	xì	connection; tie	17.2
辛	xīn	suffering	23.2
完	wán	finish	12.2
忘	wàng	forget	13.1
位	wèi	M (polite)	6.1
我	wǒ	I; me	1.1
希	xī	hope	8.2
言	yán	word	13.1
医／醫	yī	doctor; medicine	2.2
应／應	yīng	should; ought to	15.2
迎／迎	yíng	welcome	22.1
邮／郵	yóu	mail; post	19.1
员／員	yuán	personnel	9.1
园／園	yuán	garden	10.1
远／遠	yuǎn	far; distant	14.1
运／運	yùn	carry; transport	14.1
张／張	zhāng	M; (a surname)	2.1
找	zhǎo	look for; seek	4.2
折	zhé	break; discount	21.1
这／這	zhè(i)	this	2.1
针／針	zhēn	needle	16.1
证／證	zhèng	evidence	13.1
纸／紙	zhǐ	paper	18.1
助	zhù	assist	7.1
住	zhù	live	14.1
走	zǒu	walk	11.1
足	zú	foot	20.2
坐	zuò	sit	5.1
作	zuò	work; do	5.1

8

哎／哎	āi	Excl.	14.2
爸	bà	dad	2.1
拌	bàn	mix	12.2
抱	bào	hold; hug	20.2
杯	bēi	cup; glass	5.1
备／備	bèi	prepare	18.1
表	biǎo	outside; form	15.1
参／參	cān	participate	17.1
厕／廁	cè	lavatory; toilet	16.1
衬／襯	chèn	lining	9.1
单／單	dān	one; single; odd	14.2
担／擔	dān	carry	20.2
到	dào	arrive	6.1
的	de	P	2.1
典	diǎn	standard work	13.2
店	diàn	store shop	14.1
定	dìng	decide; fix; set	15.2
法	fǎ	method; way	7.1
房／房	fáng	house; room	17.2
放	fàng	put in; add	12.1
非	fēi	not; no	18.2
服	fú	clothing	9.1
该／該	gāi	should; ought to	15.2
狗	gǒu	dog	15.2
刮／颳	guā	blow	22.2
拐／拐	guǎi	turn	14.2
国／國	guó	country	1.2
果	guǒ	fruit; result	13.2
和	hé	and	2.2
河	hé	river	22.1
话／話	huà	speech	6.1
货／貨	huò	merchandise	9.1
或	huò	or	11.1
季	jì	season	22.1
金	jīn	(a surname); gold	14.1
经／經	jīng	pass through	8.1

京	jīng	capital	14.2
具／俱	jù	all; complete	18.1
苦／苦	kǔ	bitterness; pain	23.2
泪／淚	lèi	tear	16.2
练／練	liàn	practice; drill	6.2
林	lín	(a surname); forest	15.1
录／錄	lù	record	7.2
码／碼	mǎ	number	17.2
卖／賣	mài	sell	12.2
姆	mǔ	*nurse; *maid	15.2
念／唸	niàn	read	7.2
怕	pà	fear; be afraid	20.1
拍	pāi	racket; slap	20.1
其	qí	he; she; it; they	13.1
衫	shān	shirt	9.1
绍／紹	shào	carry on	5.1
舍	shè	house	8.1
实／實	shí	reality; fact	13.1
始	shǐ	begin	7.2
事	shì	matter; affair	3.2
视／視	shì	view	4.1
试／試	shì	try	6.1
饰／飾	shì	decorations	19.2
受	shòu	bear; receive	20.1
所(所)	suǒ	*so; place	4.1
图／圖	tú	drawing	5.2
往	wàng	towards	14.2
味	wèi	flavor	12.1
卧／臥	wò	lie (down)	18.1
物	wù	thing; matter	15.2
现／現	xiàn	present	3.2
线／線	xiàn	line	11.1
些	xiē	some	12.1
姓	xìng	surname	1.1
学／學	xué	study	1.2
押	yā	give as security	18.2
夜	yè	night	7.2
宜	yí	suitable	9.1
易	yì	easy	7.1
英／英	yīng	*England	2.2
泳	yǒng	swim	20.1
鱼／魚	yú	fish	12.2
雨	yǔ	rain	10.1
直(直)	zhí	straight	14.2
治	zhì	govern	22.2
周／週	zhōu	week	4.1
转／轉	zhuǎn	turn	21.2

9

帮／幫	bāng	help	6.2
保	bǎo	protect	16.2
便	biàn	convenient	6.1
茶／茶	chá	tea	5.1
查	chá	inspect; examine	16.1
差／差	chà	wanting; short of	23.1
城	chéng	city; town	14.2
除／除	chú	except	8.2
穿	chuān	wear	9.1
春	chūn	spring	10.2
带／帶	dài	belt; tape	13.1
点／點	diǎn	dot; o'clock	3.1
罚／罰	fá	fine; punish	13.2
费／費	fèi	spend; take (effort)	17.1
封	fēng	M (for letters)	8.2
复／復	fù	duplicate	7.1
钢／鋼	gāng	steel	15.2
给／給	gěi	give	5.1
挂／掛	guà	hang	19.1
贵／貴	guì	honorable	1.1
孩	hái	child	2.1
很	hěn	very	3.2
候	hòu	wait	4.1
活	huó	live	14.1
济／濟	jì	help; benefit	22.2
架	jià	frame; shelf	18.2

将／將	jiāng	going to	15.2
饺／餃	jiǎo	dumpling	12.1
觉／覺	jiào	feel; reckon	4.2
觉／覺	jué	feel; reckon	4.2
看	kàn	see; look	4.1
客	kè	guest	4.1
俩／倆	liǎ	M; two (people)	17.1
亮／亮	liàng	bright	5.1
律	lǜ	law; rule	2.2
洛	luò	(name of a river)	21.2
美	měi	beautiful	1.2
面	miàn	face; side	14.2
哪／哪	nǎ / něi	which	5.1
南	nán	south	14.2
胖	pàng	fat	20.1
便	pián	*inexpensive	9.1
前	qián	front; before	8.1
亲／親	qīn	related by blood	22.1
秋	qiū	autumn; fall	10.2
拾	shí	pick up	23.1
是	shì	be	1.2
室	shì	room	6.1
适／適	shì	suit; fit	9.2
首	shǒu	head	19.2
树／樹	shù	tree	22.1
顺／順	shùn	the same direction	23.1
说／說	shuō	speak	6.2
思	sī	think	4.2
送／送	sòng	deliver	11.1
虽／雖	suī	though; while	9.2
贴／貼	tiē	paste on; stick on	19.1
洗	xǐ	wash	8.1
险／險	xiǎn	danger; risk	16.2
香	xiāng	fragrant	21.2
信	xìn	letter	8.2
星	xīng	star	3.1
须／須	xū	must	13.2
养／養	yǎng	raise	18.2
要	yào	want	5.1
药／藥	yào	medicine	16.1
姨	yí	aunt	22.1
音	yīn	sound; music	4.1
语／語	yǔ	language	7.1
怎	zěn	*how	3.1
政	zhèng	politics	22.2
指	zhǐ	finger	15.2
钟／鐘	zhōng	clock	3.1
种／種	zhǒng	kind; type	16.1
重	zhòng	serious; heavy	16.2
祝	zhù	wish	8.2
昨	zuó	yesterday	4.1

10

啊／啊	a	P	6.2
爱／愛	ài	love	15.2
班	bān	class	15.1
被	bèi	Preposition	20.2
笔／筆	bǐ	pen	7.1
病	bìng	illness	16.1
部／部	bù	part; section	22.2
称／稱	chēng	weigh	23.1
都／都	dōu	all; both	2.2
都／都	dū	capital	22.2
顿／頓	dùn	M (for occurances)	21.1
饿／餓	è	be hungry	12.1
烦／煩	fán	bother	11.1
赶／趕	gǎn	hurry; rush	16.2
高	gāo	tall	2.1
哥	gē	older brother	2.2
海	hǎi	sea	10.1
航	háng	boat; ship	21.1
换／換	huàn	change	9.2
家	jiā	family; home	2.2
家／傢	jiā	*furniture	18.1

健／健	jiàn	healthy; strong	16.2
较／較	jiào	compare	22.2
借	jiè	borrow	13.1
紧／緊	jǐn	tight	11.2
酒	jiǔ	wine	5.1
剧／劇	jù	play; opera	17.2
课／課	kè	class; lesson	6.1
哭	kū	cry	23.1
离／離	lí	from; away	14.1
凉／涼	liáng	cool	10.2
留	liú	leave (behind)	13.1
流	liú	flow; shed	16.2
旅	lǚ	travel	17.2
拿	ná	take	16.2
难／難	nán	difficult; hard	7.1
脑／腦	nǎo	brain	8.1
能	néng	be able	8.2
旁	páng	side	14.1
瓶	píng	bottle	5.2
起	qǐ	rise	5.1
钱／錢	qián	money	9.1
请／請	qǐng	please; invite	1.1
热／熱	rè	hot	10.2
容	róng	hold; contain	7.1
烧／燒	shāo	burn; cook	12.2
谁／誰	shéi	who	2.1
速／速	sù	speed	11.2
素	sù	white; plain	12.1
套	tào	suite/set	18.1
特	tè	special; particular	20.2
疼	téng	be painful	16.1
调／調	tiáo	change to; adjust	20.2
铁／鐵	tiě	iron	11.1
途／途	tú	road; way	23.1
夏	xià	summer	10.2
校	xiào	school	5.1
笑	xiào	laugh	8.2
验／驗	yàn	examine; check	13.1
样／樣	yàng	kind	3.1
预／預	yù	prepare	7.1
圆／圓	yuán	round	20.2
站	zhàn	stand; station	11.1
涨／漲	zhǎng	rise	21.2
真(眞)	zhēn	true; real	7.2
准／準	zhǔn	accurate	18.2
桌	zhuō	table	12.1
租	zū	rent	11.1
座	zuò	M (for bridges, etc.)	22.1

11

猜	cāi	guess	16.2
菜／菜	cài	vegetable; dish	12.1
着／著	zhe	P	14.2
常	cháng	often	4.1
唱	chàng	sing	4.1
道／道	dào	road; way	6.2
得	dé	obtain; get	4.2
得	de	P	7.1
得	děi	must; have to	6.1 (4.2)
第	dì	(ordinal prefix)	7.1
啡	fēi	*coffee	5.1
够／夠	gòu	enough	12.1
馆／館	guǎn	accommodations	5.2
惯／慣	guàn	be used to	8.2
黄(黃)	huáng	yellow	9.1
寄	jì	mail; send by mail	19.1
假	jià	vacation	11.1
检／檢	jiǎn	inspect; examine	16.1
减／減	jiǎn	reduce; decrease	21.1
教(敎)	jiāo	teach	7.1
教(敎)	jiào	education	8.1
脚／腳	jiǎo	foot	20.2
接	jiē	meet; receive	15.1
康	kāng	well-being; health	16.2

啦	lā	P	22.1
累	lèi	be tired	23.2
理	lǐ	tidy up	17.2
脸／臉	liǎn	face	15.2
聊	liáo	chat	5.2
绿／綠	lǜ	green	11.1
麻	má	hemp; numb	11.1
敏	mǐn	quick; nimble	16.2
您	nín	you (polite)	1.1
盘／盤	pán	plate; dish	12.1
啤	pí	*beer	5.1
票	piào	ticket	11.1
婆	pó	old woman	22.1
戚	qī	relative	22.1
清	qīng	clear; clean	8.2
球	qiú	ball	4.1
盛	shèng	flourishing	21.2
售	shòu	sell	9.1
宿	sù	stay	8.1
随／隨	suí	follow	23.1
弹／彈	tán	play	15.2
探	tàn	visit	23.1
甜	tián	sweet	12.2
停	tíng	park; stop	23.1
望／望	wàng	hope; wish	8.2
象／象	xiàng	appearance	17.1
续／續	xù	continue; extend	13.2
雪／雪	xuě	snow	22.1
淹	yān	flood; submerge	20.1
眼	yǎn	eye	14.2
痒／癢	yǎng	itch	16.2
银／銀	yín	silver	19.2
营／營	yíng	operate; run	19.1
职／職	zhí	duty; job	13.1
做	zuò	do	2.2

12

棒	bàng	strong; good	20.2
超	chāo	exceed; surpass	23.1
裤／褲	kù	pants	9.1
程	chéng	rule; order; journey	21.1
厨／廚	chú	kitchen	18.1
登	dēng	board	23.1
等	děng	wait	6.1
傅	fù	teacher	12.2
港	gǎng	port; harbor	21.2
韩／韓	hán	(a surname); Korea	21.2
喝	hē	drink	5.1
黑	hēi	black	9.2
景	jǐng	scenery; scene	22.1
就	jiù	just	6.1
渴	kě	thirsty	12.1
跑	pǎo	run	20.1
期	qī	period (of time)	3.1
琴	qín	piano	15.2
然	rán	like that; so	9.2
剩	shèng	remain	13.1
舒	shū	stretch	10.2
属／屬	shǔ	belong to	15.2
暑	shǔ	heat; hot weather	15.2
提	tí	carry; raise	14.2
湾／灣	wān	strait; bay	10.2
晚	wǎn	evening; late	3.1
喂	wèi	Hello!; Hey!	6.1
喜	xǐ	like; happy	3.1
谢／謝	xiè	thank	3.1
椅	yǐ	chair	18.2
游	yóu	swim; travel	20.1
游／遊	yóu	travel; tour	22.2
寓	yù	reside; live	18.1
越	yuè	exceed; overstep	16.2
最	zuì	most	8.2

13

搬	bān	move	18.1
楚	chǔ	clear; neat	8.2
错／錯	cuò	wrong; error	4.2
跟	gēn	with	6.2
滑	huá	slide	22.1
简／簡	jiǎn	simple	20.1
睛	jīng	eyeball	14.2
蓝／藍	lán	blue	11.1
裏	裡	里	lǐ	inside	7.1
楼／樓	lóu	floor; storey	13.1
路	lù	road; way	11.2
满／滿	mǎn	full	22.1
暖	nuǎn	warm	10.1
签／簽	qiān	sign	21.1
输／輸	shū	lose (a game, etc.)	20.2
睡	shuì	sleep	4.2
跳	tiào	jump	4.1
腿／腿	tuǐ	leg	15.2
碗	wǎn	bowl	12.1
想	xiǎng	think	4.2
像／像	xiàng	image	10.1
新	xīn	new	8.1
意	yì	meaning	4.2
赢／贏	yíng	win (a game, etc.)	20.2
照	zhào	shine	2.1

14

鼻	bí	nose	15.2
腐	fǔ	rotten; stale	12.1
歌	gē	song	4.1
精	jīng	essence	12.1
静／靜	jìng	quiet	18.2
辣	là	spicy; hot	12.1
慢	màn	slow	7.1
漂	piào	*pretty	5.1
赛／賽	sài	game; match	20.2
瘦	shòu	thin	23.2
酸	suān	sour	12.1
算	suàn	calculate; figure	4.2
舞	wǔ	dance	4.1
鲜／鮮	xiān	fresh	19.2
演	yǎn	show; perform	17.1
愿／願	yuàn	be willing	20.1

15

醋	cù	vinegar	12.2
聪／聰	cōng	acute hearing	15.2
懂／懂	dǒng	understand	7.1
篇	piān	M (for articles)	8.1
躺	tǎng	lie down	16.1
踢	tī	kick	20.2
题／題	tí	topic; question	6.1
箱	xiāng	box; case; trunk	23.1
鞋	xié	shoes	9.2
颜／顏	yán	face; countenance	9.1
影	yǐng	shadow	4.1
镇／鎮	zhèn	town	22.1

16

餐	cān	meal	8.1
糕	gāo	cake	10.2
篮／籃	lán	basket	20.1
糖	táng	sugar	12.2
醒	xǐng	wake up	23.1
澡	zǎo	bath	8.1
整	zhěng	neat; tidy	17.2
嘴	zuǐ	mouth	15.2

17

糟	zāo	messy	10.2

Integrated Chinese I (Parts 1 & 2)
English-Chinese Glossary

A

a bit *aux.* 一點兒 (一点儿) yìdiǎnr IC1a
able *aux.* 能 néng IC1a
about to *adv.* 快 kuài IC1a
accustom to *v.* 習慣 (习惯) xíguàn IC1a, 慣 (惯) guàn IC1b
activity *n.* 活動 (活动) huódòng IC1b, ~ center *n.* 活動中心 (活动中心) huódòng zhōngxīn IC1b
add *v.* 放 fàng IC1b; 加 jiā IC1b
additional *adv.* 還有 (还有) háiyǒu IC1a
adjust *v.* 調 (调) tiáo IC1b
advertisement *n.* 廣告 (广告) guǎnggào IC1b
affair *n.* 事 shì IC1a
afraid (of) *v.* 怕 pà IC1b
after *adv-t.* 以後 (以后) yǐhòu IC1a
afternoon *adv-t.* 下午 xiàwǔ IC1a
afterwards *adv-t.* 以後 (以后) yǐhòu IC1b
again *adv.* 又 yòu IC1a, 再 zài IC1a
age *n.* 歲 (岁) suì IC1a
ago *ph.* 早就 zǎojiù IC1b
ahead *n.* 前 qián IC1b, *adv-l.* 前面 qiánmian IC1b
airline (company) *n.* 航空公司 hángkōng gōngsī IC1b
airplane *n.* 飛機 (飞机) fēijī IC1a
airport *n.* (飛) 機場 [(飞) 机场] (fēi)jīchǎng IC1a
alike *adj.* 一樣 (一样) yíyàng IC1a; *adv.* 同 tóng IC1b
alive *v.* 活 huó IC1b
all *adv.* 都 (都) dōu IC1a, IC1b
all out *adv.* 好好(兒) [好好(儿)] hǎohāo(r) IC1b
all right *adj.* 行 xíng IC1a
allergic *gr.* 過敏 (过敏) guòmǐn IC1b
allow *v.* 讓 (让) ràng IC1a, 許 (许) xǔ IC1b
almost *adv.* 差不多 (差不多) chàbuduō IC1b
already *adv.* 已經 (已经) yǐjīng IC1a
also *adv.* 還有 (还有) háiyǒu IC1a, IC1b; 也 yě IC1a
although *conj.* 雖然 (虽然) suīrán IC1a
altogether *adv.* 一共 yígòng IC1a
always *adv.* 老是 lǎoshi IC1b
American style *adj.* 美式 Měishì IC1b
American *n.* 美國人 (美国人) Měiguórén IC1a
ancestral home *n.* 老家 lǎojiā IC1b
and *conj.* 跟 gēn IC1a, 和 hé IC1a
animal *n.* 動物 (动物) dòngwù IC1b
anxious *adj.* 急 jí IC1b
apartment *n.* 公寓 gōngyù IC1b
are *v.* 有 yǒu IC1a
arrive *v.* 到 dào IC1a, *vc.* 來到 (来到) lái dào IC1b
ask *v.* 問 (问) wèn IC1a, ~ for directions *vo.* 問路 (问路) wènlù IC1b
at *prep.* 在 zài IC1a
attend college/university *vo.* 上大學 (上大学) shàng dàxué IC1b
attendant *n.* 服務員 (服务员) fúwùyuán IC1b
audio tape *n.* 錄音帶 (录音带) lùyīndài IC1b
aunt *n.* 阿姨 (阿姨) āyí IC1b
automobile *n.* 車 (车) chē IC1a
autumn *n.* 秋天 qiūtiān IC1a
autumn leaves *n.* 紅葉 (红叶) hóngyè IC1a
aviation *n.* 航空 hángkōng IC1b
away *prep.* 離 (离) lí IC1b
awhile *adv.* 一下 yí xià IC1a

B

back and forth *n.* 來回 (来回) láihuí IC1b
bad *adj.* 壞 (坏) huài IC1b
bad luck *adj.* 糟糕 zāogāo IC1a
baggage *n.* 行李 xíngli IC1b
ball[1] *n.* 球 qiú IC1a
ball[2] *n.* 舞會 (舞会) wǔhuì IC1b
bank *n.* 銀行 (银行) yínháng IC1b
barely *adj.* 差一點 (差一点) chàyidiǎn IC1b
basketball *n.* 籃球 (篮球) lánqiú IC1b
bathe *v.* 洗澡 xǐzǎo IC1a
bathroom *n.* 廁所 (厕所) cèsuǒ IC1b, *n.* 洗澡間 (洗澡间) xǐzǎojiān IC1b
be *v.* 是 shì IC1a, 當 (当) dāng IC1b
be (there) *v.* 在 zài IC1a
be going to *aux.* 要 yào IC1a
be like *adv.* 好像 (好像) hǎoxiàng IC1b, *v.* 像 (像) xiàng IC1b
be overweight *vc.* 超重 chāo zhòng IC1b
be painful *v.* 疼 téng IC1b
be willing *aux.* 願意 (愿意) yuànyì 20.1
be windy *vo.* 颳風 (刮风) guā fēng IC1b
beancurd *n.* 豆腐 dòufu IC1b
bear *v.* 受 shòu IC1b
beautiful *adj.* 美 měi IC1b
because *conj.* 因為 (因为) yīnwei IC1a
become *v.* 成 chéng IC1b
bed *n.* 床 chuáng IC1a
bedroom *n.* 臥室 (卧室) wòshì IC1b
beef *n.* 牛肉 niúròu IC1b
beer *n.* 啤酒 píjiǔ IC1a
before *adv.* 先 xiān IC1a, *adv-t.* 以前 yǐqián IC1a

before long *adv.* 快 kuài IC1a
begin *v.* 開始 (开始) kāishǐ IC1a
beginning *n.* 開始 (开始) kāishǐ IC1a, *adv.* 初 chū IC1b
belong to *v.* 屬 (属) shǔ IC1b
best *adv.* 最好 zuìhǎo IC1a
better *conj.* 還是 (还是) háishi IC1a
big *adj.* 大 dà IC1a
birthday *n.* 生日 shēngrì IC1a
black *n.* 黑 hēi IC1a
bloom/blossom abundantly *vc.* 開滿 (开满) kāi mǎn IC1b
blow (of the wind) *v.* 颳 (刮) guā IC1b, *vo.* 颳風 (刮风) guā fēng IC1b
blue *n.* 藍 (蓝) lán IC1a
boarding pass *n.* 登機證 (登机证) dēngjīzhèng IC1b
body *n.* 身體 (身体) shēntǐ IC1b
book *n.* 書 (书) shū IC1a
book (a ticket, a hotel room, etc.) *v.* 訂 (订) dìng IC1b
bookshelf *n.* 書架 (书架) shūjià IC1b
bookstore *n.* 書店 (书店) shūdiàn IC1b
born *v.* 生 shēng IC1a
borrow *v.* 借 jiè IC1b
both *adv.* 都 (都) dōu IC1a
bottle *n.* 瓶 píng IC1a
bow *n.* 弓 gōng Rad, ~ (drawn) *n.* 張 (张) zhāng IC1a
bowl *n.* 碗 wǎn IC1b
boy *n.* 男孩子 nánháizi IC1a
brain *n.* 腦 (脑) nǎo IC1a
braise(d) in soy sauce *vc./adj.* 紅燒 (红烧) hóngshāo IC1b
breakfast *n.* 早飯 (早饭) zǎofàn IC1a
bright *adj.* 聰明 (聪明) cōngmíng IC1b
bring *v.* 帶 (带) dài IC1b
bring with one *vo.* 隨身 (随身) suíshēn IC1b
brown *n.* 咖啡色 kāfēisè IC1a
bus *n.* 公共汽車 (公共汽车) gōnggòng qìchē IC1a
business *n.* 事 shì IC1a
busy *adj.* 忙 máng IC1a
but *conj.* 不過 (不过) búguò IC1a, 但是 dànshi IC1a, 可是 kěshì IC1a
buy *v.* 買 (买) mǎi IC1a

C

cab *n.* 出租汽車 (出租汽车) chūzū qìchē IC1a
cafeteria *n.* 餐廳 (餐厅) cāntīng IC1a
call *vo.* 打電話 (打电话) dǎ diànhuà IC1a; *v.* 叫 jiào IC1a
can *v.* 會 (会) huì IC1a, 能 néng IC1a, *adv.* 可以 kěyǐ IC1a
capital *n.* 首都 (首都) shǒudū IC1b
car *n.* 車 (车) chē IC1a
card *n.* 卡 (片) kǎ(piàn) IC1b
careful *v.* 小心 xiǎoxīn IC1b
carry *v.* 拿 ná IC1b
carry (with the arm down) *v.* 提 tí IC1b
carry on one's person *vo.* 隨身 (随身) suíshēn IC1b
carry or hold in the arms *v.* 抱 bào IC1b
cause *v.* 讓 (让) ràng IC1a
celebrate *v.* 慶祝 (庆祝) qìngzhù IC1b;
~ (a birthday, a holiday, etc.) *v.* 過 (过) guò IC1b,
~ a birthday *vo.* 過生日 (过生日) guò shēngrì IC1b,
cent *n.* 分 fēn IC1a
center *n.* 中心 zhōngxīn IC1b
certainly *adv.* 一定 yídìng IC1b
chair *n.* 椅子 yǐzi IC1b
change *v.* 換 (换) huàn IC1a, ~ (a channel) *v.* 調 (调) tiáo IC1b
change planes *vo.* 轉機 (转机) zhuǎn jī IC1b
channel (TV, radio) *n.* 台 tái IC1b
character *n.* 字 zì IC1a
chat *vo.* 聊天(兒) [聊天 (儿)] liáo tiān(r) IC1a, *v.* 聊 liáo IC1b
cheap *adj.* 便宜 piányi IC1a
check2 *n.* 支票 zhīpiào IC1b
check in (baggage) *v.* 托運 (托运) tuōyùn IC1b
cheque *n.* 支票 zhīpiào IC1b
child *n.* 孩子 háizi IC1a
Chinese *n.* 中國人 (中国人) Zhōngguórén IC1a, ~ (language) 中文 Zhōngwén IC1a
Chinese character(s) *n.* 漢字 (汉字) Hànzì IC1a
Chinese dollar *n.* 元 yuán IC1b
Chinese food *n.* 中餐 Zhōngcān IC1b
city *n.* 城 chéng IC1b, 城市 chéngshì IC1b
class *n.* 課 (课) kè IC1a, 班 bān IC1b
classmate *n.* 同學 (同学) tóngxué IC1a
classroom *n.* 教室 jiàoshì IC1a
clean up *v.* 打掃 (打扫) dǎsǎo IC1b

clear *adj.* 清楚 qīngchu IC1a
clerk *n.* 營業員 (营业员) yíngyèyuán IC1b
clever *adj.* 聰明 (聪明) cōngming IC1b
clock *n.* 鐘 (钟) zhōng IC1a
close *v.* 關 (关) guān IC1b,
~ (a door) *vo.* 關門 (关门) guān mén IC1b;
v. 閉 (闭) bì IC1b, *vc.* 閉著 (闭着) bìzhe IC1b
clothes *n.* 衣服 yīfu IC1a
clothing *n.* 衣服 yīfu IC1a
coffee *n.* 咖啡 kāfēi IC1a, ~ (color) *n.* 咖啡色 kāfēisè IC1a
cola *n.* 可樂 (可乐) kělè IC1a
cold *adj.* 冷 lěng IC1a
cold and dressed with sauce (of food) *n.* 涼拌 (凉拌) liángbàn IC1b
college *n.* 大學 (大学) dàxué IC1a, ~ student *n.* 大學生 (大学生) dàxuéshēng IC1a
color *n.* 顏色 (颜色) yánsè IC1a
come *v.* 來 (来) lái IC1a,
~ to *vc.* 來到 (来到) lái dào IC1b,
~ back *vc.* 回來 (回来) huílai IC1a,
~ in 進來 (进来) jìnlai IC1a
come with *v.* 帶 (带) dài IC1b
comfortable *adj.* 舒服 shūfu IC1a
company *n.* 公司 gōngsī IC1b
compare *v.* 比 bǐ IC1a
competition *n.* 賽 (赛) sài IC1b
computer *n. coll.* 電腦 (电脑) diànnǎo IC1a
concert *n.* 音樂會 (音乐会) yīnyuèhuì IC1a
consign for shipment *v.* 托運 (托运) tuōyùn IC1b
convenient *adj.* 方便 fāngbiàn IC1a
cook *vc.* 做飯 (做饭) zuò fàn IC1b
cooked rice *n.* 米飯 (米饭) mǐfàn IC1b
cool *adj.* 涼快 (凉快) liángkuai IC1a
correct *adj.* 對 (对) duì IC1a, IC1b
cost (money) *vo.* 花錢 (花钱) huā qián IC1b,
~ (time) *vo.* 花時間 (花时间) huā shíjiān IC1b
cost *v.* 要 yào IC1b
countryside *n.* 鄉下 (乡下) xiāngxià IC1b
couple *n.* 兩 (两) liǎng IC1a
course (of food) *n.* 菜 (菜) cài IC1b
course load *n.* 功課 (功课) gōngkè IC1a
cousin (younger male) *n.* 表弟 biǎodì IC1b,
(older male) ~ 表哥 biǎogē IC1b,
(older female) ~ *n.* 表姐 biǎojiě IC1b
cow *n.* 牛 niú IC1b
credit *n.* 信用 xìnyòng IC1b, ~ card *n.* 信用卡 xìnyònkǎ IC1b
cry *v.* 哭 kū IC1b
cucumber *n.* 黃瓜 (黄瓜) huángguā IC1b
culture *n.* 文化 wénhuà IC1b
cup *n.* 杯 bēi IC1a
currency *n.* 幣 (币) bì IC1b
cut price *vo.* 減價 (减价) jiǎn jià IC1b
cute *adj.* 可愛 (可爱) kě'ài IC1b

D

dad *n.* 爸爸 bàba IC1a
dance *vo.* 跳舞 tiào wǔ IC1a, *n.* 舞 wǔ IC1a, 舞會 (舞会) wǔhuì IC1b
dangerous *adj.* 危險 (危险) wēixiǎn IC1b
daughter *n.* 女兒 (女儿) nǚ'ér IC1a
day *n.* 日 rì IC1a, 天 tiān IC1a, 號 (号) hào IC1a
day before *adv-t.* 前一天 qián yì tiān IC1b
day after tomorrow *adv-t.* 後天 (后天) hòutiān IC1b
definitely *adv.* 一定 yídìng IC1b
delicious *adj.* 好吃 hǎochī IC1b
depart *v.* 走 zǒu IC1b
deposit money *vo.* 存錢 (存钱) cún qián IC1b
desire *v.* 要 yào IC1a
desk *n.* 書桌 (书桌) shūzhuō IC1b
diary *n.* 日記 (日记) rìjì IC1a
dictionary *n.* 字典 zìdiǎn IC1b
die *v.* 死 sǐ IC1b
different places *n.* 各地 gè dì IC1b
difficult *adj.* 難 (难) nán IC1a
diligent *adj.* 用功 yònggōng IC1b
dime *n.* 毛 máo IC1a
dining room *n.* 餐廳 (餐厅) cāntīng IC1a
dining table *n.* 飯桌 (饭桌) fànzhuō IC1b
dinner *n.* 晚飯 (晚饭) wǎnfàn IC1a
discount *vo.* 打折 (扣) dǎ zhé(kòu) IC1b, *vo.* 減價 (减价) jiǎn jià IC1b
dish *n.* 菜 (菜) cài IC1b
distinct *adj.* 分明 fēnmíng IC1b
do *v.* 做 zuò IC1a, 辦 (办) bàn IC1b
doctor *n.* 醫生 (医生) yīshēng IC1a
dog *n.* 狗 gǒu IC1b
dollar *n.* 塊 (块) kuài IC1a
don't *v.* 別 bié IC1a
door *n.* 門 (门) mén IC1b
doorway *n.* 門口 (门口) ménkǒu IC1b
dormitory *n.* 宿舍 sùshè IC1a
downstairs *adv-l.* 樓下 (楼下) lóuxià IC1b

drink *v.* 喝 hē IC1a
drive *v.* 開 (开) kāi IC1a, *vo.* 開車 (开车) kāi chē IC1a
drown to death *vc.* 淹死 yān sǐ IC1b
dumplings *n.* 餃子 (饺子) jiǎozi IC1b

E

each *adv.* 每 měi IC1a, 各 gè IC1b
early *adj.* 早 zǎo IC1a, *adv.* 才 cái IC1b
east *n.* 東 (东) dōng IC1b
easy *adj.* 容易 róngyì IC1a, *adv.* 好 hǎo IC1b
eat *v.* 吃 chī IC1a, ~ (a meal) *vo.* 吃飯 (吃饭) chī fàn IC1a
economy *n.* 經濟 (经济) jīngjì IC1b
embarrassed *ph.* 不好意思 bù hǎoyìsi IC1a
English *n.* 英文 (英文) Yīngwén IC1a
enough *adj.* 夠 (够) gòu IC1b
enter *v.* 進 (进) jìn IC1a
even *conj.* 連 (连) lián IC1b
even more *adv.* 更 gèng IC1a
evening *n.* 晚上 wǎnshang IC1a
every *adv.* 每 měi IC1a, 各 gè IC1b,
~ day *adv-t.* 每天 měitiān IC1a
everybody *n.* 大家 dàjiā IC1a
examine *v.* 檢查 (检查) jiǎnchá IC1b
example *n.* 比方 bǐfang IC1b
exceedingly *vc.* 死 sǐ IC1b
exchange *v.* 換 (换) huàn IC1a
exhausted *vc./adj.* 累壞 (累坏) lèihuài IC1b
expenses *n.* 費 (费) fèi IC1b
expensive *adj.* 貴 (贵) guì IC1a
experiment *n./v.* 實驗 (实验) shíyàn IC1b
express letter *n.* 快信 kuàixìn IC1b
extraordinarily *adv.* 非常 fēicháng IC1b
extremely *adv.* 極 (了) [极(了)] jí(le) IC1b, *vc.* 死 sǐ IC1b
eye *n.* 眼睛 yǎnjing IC1b

F

face *n.* 臉 (脸) liǎn IC1b
fall *n.* 秋天 qiūtiān IC1a
family *n.* 家 jiā IC1a
fantastic *adj. coll.* 棒 bàng IC1b
far *adj.* 遠 (远) yuǎn IC1b
fast *adj.* 快 kuài IC1a
fat *adj.* 胖 pàng IC1b
father *n.* 父(親) [父(亲)] fù(qin) IC1b
father and mother *n.* 父母 fùmǔ IC1b
father's elder brother *n.* 伯伯 bóbo IC1b
favor *vo.* 幫忙 (帮忙) bāng máng IC1a
fear *v.* 怕 pà 20.1
fee *n.* 費 (费) fèi IC1b
feel *v.* 覺得 (觉得) juéde IC1a
female *n.* 女 nǚ IC1a
few *n.* 幾 (几) jǐ IC1a
field *n.* 場 (场) chǎng IC1a, IC1b
fifteen minutes *adv-t.* 刻 kè IC1a
final *n.* 最後 (最后) zuìhòu IC1b
finally *adv.* 最後 (最后) zuìhòu IC1a
find (successfully) *vc.* 找到 zhǎo dào IC1b
fine[1] *adj.* 好 hǎo IC1a
fine[2] *v.* 罰 (罚) fá IC1b
finger *n.* 手指 shǒuzhǐ IC1b
finish *v.* 完 wán IC1b
first *adv.* 先 xiān IC1a
fish *n.* 魚 (鱼) yú IC1b,
~ in sweet and sour sauce *n.* 糖醋魚 (糖醋鱼) tángcùyú IC1b
flow *v.* 流 liú IC1b
flower *n.* 花 (花) huā IC1b
fly *v.* 飛 (飞) fēi IC1a,
~ directly *adv.* 直飛 (直飞) zhífēi IC1b
foot *n.* 腳 (脚) jiǎo IC1b
for *prep.* 給 (给) gěi IC1a, *adv.* 為 (为) wèi IC1a
for example *ph.* 比方說 (比方说) bǐfang shuō IC1b
for the sake of *conj.* 為了 (为了) wèile IC1b
forecast *n.* 預報 (预报) yùbào IC1a
foreign country *n.* 外國 (外国) wàiguó IC1a
forget *v.* 忘 wàng IC1b
forward *n.* 前 qián IC1b
fresh *adj.* 新鮮 (新鲜) xīnxiān IC1b
friend *n.* 朋友 péngyou IC1a
from *prep.* 從 (从) cóng IC1b, 離 (离) lí IC1b
fruit *n.* 水果 shuǐguǒ IC1b,
~ juice *n.* 果汁 guǒzhī IC1b
full *adj.* 滿 (满) mǎn IC1b
furniture *n.* 傢俱 (家具) jiājù IC1b
furthermore *adv.* 還有 (还有) hái yǒu IC1b

G

game *n.* 賽 (赛) sài IC1b
get *v.* 拿 ná IC1b, 得 dé L13
get (injured or wounded) *v.* 受 shòu IC1b
get a shot *vo.* 打針 (打针) dǎ zhēn IC1b
get off *vo.* 下車 (下车) xià chē IC1a
get sick *vo.* 生病 shēngbìng IC1b

get sick (because of having eaten bad food) *vc.* 吃壞 (吃坏) chī huài IC1b
get up *vo.* 起床 qǐ chuáng IC1a
gift *n.* 禮物 (礼物) lǐwù IC1b
girl *n.* 女孩子 nǚháizi IC1a
girlfriend *n.* 女朋友 nǚpéngyou IC1b
give *v.* 給 (给) gěi IC1a
give a test/exam *v.* 考 kǎo IC1a, *vo.* 考試 (考试) kǎo shì IC1a
give birth to *v.* 生 shēng IC1a
give change *v(o).* 找 (錢) [找 (钱)] zhǎo (qián) IC1a
give a discount *vo.* 打折 (扣) [打折(扣)] dǎ zhé(kòu) IC1b
give service to *v.* 服務 (服务) fúwù IC1b
glass *n.* 杯 bēi IC1a
go *v.* 去 qù IC1a, 走 zǒu IC1a, 行 xíng IC1b, *v. coll.* 上 shàng IC1b;
~ into *vc.* 進去 (进去) jìnqu IC1b;
~ on a journey *vo.* 出門 (出门) chū mén IC1b;
~ out *vc.* 出去 chūqu IC1a
go home *vo.* 回家 huí jiā IC1a
go the same way *vo.* 同路 tóng lù IC1b
go to class *vo.* 上課 (上课) shàng kè IC1a
go to see a doctor *vo.* 看病 kàn bìng IC1b
good *adj.* 好 hǎo IC1a
grade *n.* 年級 (年级) niánjí IC1a
grammar *n.* 語法 (语法) yǔfǎ IC1a
grandfather (maternal) *n.* 外公 wàigōng IC1b ,
~ (paternal) 爺爺 (爷爷) yéye IC1b
grandmother (maternal) *n.* 外婆 wàipó IC1b
~ (paternal) 奶奶 (奶奶) nǎinai IC1b
grandson (paternal) *n.* 孫子 (孙子) sūnzi IC1b
green *adj.* 綠 (绿) lǜ IC1a
grow *vc.* 長得 (长得) zhǎng de L3,
~ in such a way as to appear *vc.* 長得 (长得) zhǎngde IC1b,
guess *v.* 猜 cāi IC1b

H

habit *n.* 習慣 xíguàn IC1a
had better *adv.* 最好 zuìhǎo IC1a
hail/hire (a taxi) *v.* 叫 jiào IC1b
half *n.* 半 bàn IC1a,
~ day *adj.* 半天 bàntiān IC1b
hand *n.* 手 shǒu IC1b
handle *v.* 辦 (办) bàn IC1b
handsome *adj.* 帥 (帅) shuài IC1a
happy *adj.* 高興 (高兴) gāoxìng IC1a, 快樂 (快乐) kuàilè IC1a
hard *adj.* 辛苦 (辛苦) xīnkǔ IC1b
hard to bear *adj.* 難受 (难受) nánshòu IC1b
hard-working *adj.* 用功 yònggōng IC1b
have *v.* 有 yǒu IC1a
have a holiday/vacation *vo.* 放假 fàng jià IC1b
have a meeting *vo.* 開會 (开会) kāi huì IC1a
have a visit *v.* 玩 (兒) [玩(儿)] wán(r) IC1a
have (free) time *vo.* 有空 (兒) [有空(儿)] yǒu kòng(r) IC1a
have not *adv.* 沒 (没) méi IC1a
have summer vacation *vo.* 放暑假 fàng shǔjià IC1b
have to *aux.* 得 děi IC1a
he *pron.* 他 tā IC1a
health *n.* 健康 jiànkāng IC1b, 身體 (身体) shēntǐ IC1b,
~ insurance *n.* 健康保險 (健康保险) jiànkāng bǎoxiǎn IC1b
help *v.* 幫 (帮) bāng IC1a, 幫助 (帮助) bāngzhù IC1a, *vo.* 幫忙 (帮忙) bāng máng IC1a
here *pron.* 這兒 (这儿) zhèr IC1a, 這裡 (这里) zhèlǐ IC1b
high *adj.* 高 gāo IC1a, IC1b
high-speed *adj.* 高速 (高速) gāosù IC1a
highway *n.* 高速公路 (高速公路) gāosù gōnglù IC1a, 公路 gōnglù IC1a
hill *n.* 山 shān IC1b
him *pron.* 他 tā IC1a
hit *v.* 打 dǎ IC1a
hold (a meeting, party, etc.) *v.* 開 (开) kāi IC1a
hold or carry in the arms *v.* 抱 bào IC1b
holiday *n.* 假 jià IC1b
home *n.* 家 jiā IC1a
home-style tofu *n.* 家常豆腐 jiācháng dòufu IC1b
homesick *vo.* 想家 xiǎng jiā IC1b
hometown *n.* 家鄉 (家乡) jiāxiāng IC1b, 老家 lǎojiā IC1b
homework *n.* 功課 (功课) gōngkè IC1a
honorable *adj.* 貴 (贵) guì IC1a
hope *v.* 希望 xīwàng IC1a
host *vo.* 請客 (请客) qǐng kè IC1a
hot *adj.* 熱 (热) rè IC1a, 辣 là IC1b
hot-and-sour soup *n.* 酸辣湯 (酸辣汤) suānlàtāng IC1b

hour *n.* 小時 (小时) xiǎoshí IC1b, 鐘頭 (钟头) zhōngtóu IC1b
house *n.* 房子 fángzi IC1b
how *quest. pron.* 怎麼 (怎么) zěnme IC1a
how come *quest. pron.* 怎麼 (怎么) zěnme IC1a
how long *adv.* 多久 duō jiǔ IC1b
however *conj.* 不過 (不过) búguò IC1a
hundred *n.* 百 bǎi IC1a
hungry *adj.* 餓 (饿) è IC1b
hurry *adv.* 趕快 (赶快) gǎnkuài IC1b
hurt *adj.* 疼 téng IC1b
hurt by being crushed *vc.* 壓壞 (压坏) yā huài IC1b

I

I *pron.* 我 wǒ IC1a
identification *n.* 證件 (证件) zhèngjiàn IC1b
if *conj.* 要是 yàoshi IC1a, 如果 rúguǒ IC1b
illness *n.* 病 bìng IC1b
important *adj.* 重要 zhòngyào IC1b
impression *n.* 印象 yìnxiàng IC1b
improve *vc.* 提高 tí gāo IC1b
in *adv.* 在 zài IC1a
in addition *adv.* 另外 lìngwài IC1b, 再 zài IC1b
in front of *adv-l.* 前面 qiánmian IC1b
in that case *conj.* 那麼 (那么) nàme IC1b
in the future *adv-t.* 將來 (将来) jiānglái IC1b; 以後 (以后) yǐhòu IC1b
incorrect *adj.* 不對 (不对) búduì IC1b
increase in price *vo.* 漲價 (涨价) zhǎng jià IC1b
inexpensive *adj.* 便宜 piányi IC1a
injury *n.* 傷 (伤) shāng IC1b
inside *adv-l.* 裡頭 (里头) lǐtou IC1b, *n.* 內 nèi IC1b
insurance *n.* 保險 (保险) bǎoxiǎn IC1b
intelligent *adj.* 聰明 (聪明) cōngming IC1b
interesting *adj.* 有意思 yǒu yìsi IC1a
international *adj./n.* 國際 (国际) guójì IC1b
intersection *n.* 路口 lùkǒu IC1b
introduce *v.* 介紹 (介绍) jièshào IC1a
invite *v.* 請 (请) qǐng IC1a, *vo.* 請客 (请客) qǐng kè IC1a
is *v.* 是 shì IC1a, 有 yǒu IC1a
it *pron.* 它 tā IC1b
itch *v.* 癢 (痒) yǎng IC1b
itchy *adj.* 癢 (痒) yǎng IC1b
itinerary *n.* 日程 rìchéng IC1b

J

Japanese (language) *n.* 日文 Rìwén IC1b
jewelry *n.* 首飾 (首饰) shǒushi IC1b
jog *vo.* 跑步 pǎo bù IC1b
jump *v.* 跳 tiào IC1a
just *adv.* 就 jiù IC1a, IC1b
just (indicating the immediate past) *adv.* 剛 (刚) gāng IC1b
just now *adv-t.* 剛才 (刚才) gāngcái IC1a

K

kick *v.* 踢 tī IC1b
kilogram (kg) *n.* 公斤 gōngjīn IC1b
kind *n.* 種 (种) zhǒng IC1b
king *n.* 王 wáng IC1a
kitchen *n.* 廚房 (厨房) chúfáng IC1b
know *v.* 認識 (认识) rènshi IC1a, 知道 (知道) zhīdao IC1a
know how to *aux.* 會 (会) huì IC1a

L

laboratory *n.* 實驗室 (实验室) shíyànshì IC1b
lady *n.* 小姐 xiǎojie IC1a
landlord *n.* 房東 (房东) fángdōng IC1b
language *n.* 文 wén IC1a, 語言 (语言) yǔyán IC1b
last *n.* 最後 (最后) zuìhòu IC1b
last week *adv-t.* 上個星期 (上个星期) shàngge xīngqī IC1a
late *adj.* 晚 wǎn IC1a
later *adv-t.* 後來 (后来) hòulái IC1a, 以後 (以后) yǐhòu IC1b
laugh *v.* 笑 xiào IC1a
lawyer *n.* 律師 (律师) lǜshī IC1a
leather suitcase *n.* 皮箱 píxiāng IC1b
leave behind *v.* 留 liú IC1b
left *n.* 左 zuǒ IC1b, ~ side *adv-l.* 左邊 (左边) zuǒbian IC1b
left over *v.* 剩 shèng IC1b
leftovers *n.* 剩菜 (剩菜) shèngcài IC1b
leg *n.* 腿 (腿) tuǐ IC1b
less than *adv.* 不到 bú dào IC1b
lesson *n.* 課 (课) kè IC1a
let out[1] *n.* 出租 chūzū IC1a
letter *n.* 信 xìn IC1a
liang (a Chn trad. unit of weight, =50 grams) *n.* 兩 (两) liǎng IC1b

librarian *n.* 圖書館員 (图书馆员) túshūguǎnyuán IC1b
library *n.* 圖書館 (图书馆) túshūguǎn IC1a
library card *n.* 借書證 (借书证) jièshūzhèng IC1b
library ID *n.* 借書證 (借书证) jièshūzhèng IC1b
lie *v.* 躺 tǎng IC1b,
~ down *vc.* 躺下 tǎng xià IC1b
life *n.* 生活 shēnghuó IC1b
light *n.* 燈 (灯) dēng IC1b
like *v.* 喜歡 (喜欢) xǐhuan IC1a
like this *pron.* 這樣 (这样) zhèyàng IC1a
line *n.* 線 (线) xiàn IC1a
listen *v.* 聽 (听) tīng IC1a
listening comprehension *n.* 聽力 (听力) tīnglì IC1b
little *adv.* 點兒 (点儿) diǎnr IC1a, 有一點兒 (有一点儿) yǒu yìdiǎnr IC1a; *adj.* 小 xiǎo IC1a
live *v.* 活 huó IC1b,
~ (at/in a place) *v.* 住 zhù IC1b
living room *n.* 客廳 (客厅) kètīng IC1b
long *adj.* 長 (长) cháng IC1b,
~ distance *n.* 長途 (长途) chángtú IC1b
long since *ph.* 早就 zǎojiù IC1b
long time *adv.* 好久 hǎojiǔ IC1a, *adj.* 久 jiǔ IC1a, 半天 bàntiān IC1b
look *v.* 看 kàn IC1a
look for *v.* 找 zhǎo IC1a
lose (a game, etc.) *v.* 輸 (输) shū IC1b
lovable *adj.* 可愛 (可爱) kě'ài IC1b
love *v.* 愛 (爱) ài IC1b
lunch *n.* 午飯 (午饭) wǔfàn IC1a

M

machine *n.* 機 (机) jī IC1a
mail *v.* 寄 jì 19.1
major *n.* 專業 (专业) zhuānyè IC1a
make a phone call *vo.* 打電話 (打电话) dǎ diànhuà IC1a
make an appointment *v.* 約 (约) yuē IC1a
make progress *v.* 進步 (进步) jìnbù IC1a
male *n.* 男 nán IC1a, 男的 nán de IC1a
map *n.* 地圖 (地图) dìtú IC1b
master worker *n.* 師傅 (师傅) shīfu IC1b
match *n.* 賽 (赛) sài IC1b
maternal grandfather *n.* 外公 wàigōng IC1b,
~ grandmother *n.* 外婆 wàipó IC1b
matter *n.* 事 shì IC1a
may *adv.* 可以 kěyǐ IC1a
me *pron.* 我 wǒ IC1a
meal *n.* 飯 (饭) fàn IC1a
meat *n.* 肉 ròu IC1b
medicine *n.* 藥 (药) yào IC1b
medium *adj.* 中 zhōng IC1a
meet *v.* 接 jiē IC1b
meeting *n.* 會 (会) huì IC1a
mention *vc.* 說到 (说到) shuō dào IC1b
mess *adj.* 糟糕 zāogāo IC1a
method *n.* 辦法 (办法) bànfǎ IC1b
middle *adv-l.* 中間 (中间) zhōngjiān IC1b
midnight *adv-t.* 半夜 bànyè IC1a
mile *n.* 英里 (英里) yīnglǐ IC1b
Miss *n.* 小姐 xiǎojie IC1a
miss home *vo.* 想家 xiǎng jiā IC1b
mister *n.* 先生 xiānsheng IC1a
mix *v.* 調 (调) tiáo IC1b
mom *n.* 媽媽 (妈妈) māma IC1a
moment *n.* 時候 (时候) shíhou IC1a
money *n.* 錢 (钱) qián IC1a
monosodium glutimate (MSG) *n.* 味精 wèijīng IC1b
month *n.* 月 yuè IC1a
more than *adv.* 多 duō IC1b
more or less (the same) *adv.* 差不多 (差不多) chàbuduō IC1b
moreover *adv. coll.* 再說 (再说) zàishuō IC1b
morning *adv-t.* 上午 shàngwǔ IC1a, 早上 zǎoshang IC1a
most *adv.* 最 zuì IC1a
mother *n.* 母 (親) [母 (亲)] mǔ(qin) IC1b
mother's younger sister *n.* 阿姨 (阿姨) āyí IC1b
mountain *n.* 山 shān IC1b
mouth *n.* 嘴 zuǐ IC1b
move *v.* 搬 bān IC1b
move out of *vc.* 搬出去 bān chuqu IC1b
movie *n.* 電影 (电影) diànyǐng IC1a
Mr. *n.* 先生 xiānsheng IC1a
much *adj.* 多 duō IC1a
music *n.* 音樂 (音乐) yīnyuè IC1a
must *aux.* 得 děi IC1a, *adv.* 必須 (必须) bìxū IC1b, 一定 yídìng IC1b

N

name *n.* 名字 míngzi IC1a
near *adj.* 近 (近) jìn IC1a, IC1b
nearby *adj.* 附近 (附近) fùjìn IC1b

nearly *adv.* 差不多 (差不多) chàbuduō IC1b, *adj.* 差一點 (差一点) chàyidiǎn IC1b
need *v.* 要 yào IC1a, IC1b; *n.* 必要 bìyào L13, ~ not *ph.* 不用 bú yòng IC1a
needle *n.* 針 (针) zhēn IC1b
nervous *adj.* 緊張 (紧张) jǐnzhāng IC1a
new *adj.* 新 xīn IC1a, ~ year *n.* 新年 xīnnián IC1a
new words *n.* 生詞 (生词) shēngcí IC1a
newspaper *n.* 報 (报) bào IC1a, 報紙 (报纸) bàozhǐ IC1b
next *adv.* 下 xià IC1a,
~ time *adv-t.* 下次 xià cì IC1a ,
~ week *n.* 下個星期 (下个星期) xiàge xīngqi IC1a
nice *adj.* 好 hǎo IC1a
night *adv-t.* 晚上 wǎnshang IC1a, *n.* 夜 yè IC1b
no *adv.* 不 bù IC1a
no problem *ph.* 沒問題 (没问题) méi wèntí IC1a
noisy *adj.* 吵 chǎo IC1b
noon *adv-t.* 中午 zhōngwǔ IC1a
north *n.* 北 běi IC1b
nose *n.* 鼻子 bízi IC1b
not *adv.* 不 bù IC1a, 沒 (没) méi IC1a
not bad *adj.* 不錯 (不错) búcuò IC1a
not enough room *vc.* 放不下 fàng bu xià IC1b
not until *adv.* 才 cái IC1a
novel *adj.* 新鮮 (新鲜) xīnxiān IC1b
now *adv-t.* 現在 (现在) xiànzài IC1a, 今 jīn IC1a
number *n.* 號 (号) hào IC1a, 號碼 (号码) hàomǎ IC1b

O

O.K. *adj.* 好 hǎo IC1a, 行 xíng IC1a
o'clock *n.* 點 (点) diǎn IC1a, 點鐘 (点钟) diǎnzhōng IC1a
objects *n.* 東西 (东西) dōngxi IC1a
odd *n.* 單 (单) dān IC1b
of course *adv.* 當然 (当然) dāngrán IC1b
of vegetables *adj.* 素 sù IC1b
office *n.* 辦公室 (办公室) bàngōngshì IC1a
office worker *n.* 職員 (职员) zhíyuán IC1b
often *adv.* 常常 chángcháng IC1a, *adj.* 常 cháng IC1b
old *adj.* 大 dà IC1a, 舊 (旧) jiù IC1b,
~ student *n.* 老生 lǎoshēng L1
older brother *n.* 哥哥 gēge IC1a
older sister *n.* 姐姐 jiějie IC1a
on *prep.* 在 zài IC1a
on the way *adv-l.* 路上 lùshang IC1b
one *n.* 單 (单) dān IC1b
one-way street *n.* 單行道 (单行道) dānxíngdào IC1b
one-way trip *n.* 單程 (单程) dānchéng IC1b
one bedroom and one living room *n.* 一房一廳 (一房一厅) yì fáng yì tīng IC1b
one's heart's content *adv.* 好好 (兒) [好好 (儿)] hǎohāo(r) IC1b
oneself *n.* 自己 zìjǐ IC1a
only *adv.* 只 zhǐ IC1a,
~ (indicating a small number) *adv.* 就 jiù IC1b
only then *adv.* 才 cái IC1b
open *v.* 開 (开) kāi IC1b,
~ till ... *vc.* 開到 (开到) kāi dào IC1b
opera *n.* 歌劇 (歌剧) gējù IC1b
operate *v.* 開 (开) kāi IC1a
opposite (side) *n.* 對面 (对面) duìmiàn IC1b
or *conj.* 還是 (还是) háishi IC1a, 或者 huòzhě IC1a
order *v.* 訂 (订) dìng IC1b
order dishes/food (in a restaurant) *vo.* 點菜 (点菜) diǎn cài IC1b
other *adv.* 別 (的) [別 (的)] bié (de) IC1a, *n.* 其他的 qítā de IC1b,
~ people *n.* 別人 (别人) biérén IC1b
others *n.* 別人 (别人) biérén IC1b
otherwise *conj.* 要不然 yàoburán IC1b
overdue *adj.* 過期 (过期) guòqī IC1b
ox *n.* 牛 niú IC1b

P

pack *v.* 收拾 shōushi IC1b
painful *adj.* 疼 téng IC1b
pants *n.* 褲子 (裤子) kùzi IC1a
paper *n.* 紙 (纸) zhǐ IC1b
parents *n.* 父母 fùmǔ IC1b
park[1] *n.* 公園 (公园) gōngyuán IC1a
park[2] *v.* 停 tíng IC1b,
~ (a car, bike, etc.) *vo.* 停車 (停车) tíng chē IC1b
parking lot *n.* 停車場 (停车场) tíngchēchǎng IC1b
part *n.* 部 (部) bù IC1b
pass *v.* 過 (过) guò IC1b
passport *n.* 護照 (护照) hùzhào IC1b
past few days *ph.* 這幾天 (这几天) zhè jǐ tiān IC1a
paste *v.* 貼 (贴) tiē IC1b

paternal grandfather *n.* 爺爺 (爷爷) yéye IC1b,
~ grandmother *n.* 奶奶 (奶奶) nǎinai IC1b,
~ grandson *n.* 孫子 (孙子) sūnzi IC1b
patient *n.* 病人 bìngrén IC1b
pay *vo.* 付錢 (付钱) fù qián IC1a
pen *n.* 筆 (笔) bǐ IC1a
penny *n.* 分 fēn IC1a
people *n.* 人 rén IC1a, 人民 rénmín IC1b
perform *v.* 演 yǎn IC1b
person *n.* 人 rén IC1a
pharmacy *n.* 藥店 (药店) yàodiàn IC1b
photo *n.* 照片 zhàopiàn IC1a
physician *n.* 醫生 (医生) yīshēng IC1a
piano *n.* 鋼琴 (钢琴) gāngqín IC1b
picture *n.* 照片 zhàopiàn IC1a
place *n.* 地方 dìfang IC1b, *v.* 放 fàng IC1b
plan *v.* 打算 dǎ suàn IC1b, 準備 (准备) zhǔnbèi IC1b;
n. 計劃 (计划) jìhuà IC1b
plane *n.* 飛機 (飞机) fēijī IC1a
plant *v.* 種 (种) zhòng IC1b
plate *n.* 盤 (盘) pán IC1b
play *v.* 玩 (兒) [玩 (儿)] wán(r) IC1a,
~ (a stringed musical instrument) *v.* 彈 (弹) tán IC1b,
~ ball *vo.* 打球 dǎ qiú IC1a
please *v.* 請 (请) qǐng IC1a
pleased *adj.* 高興 (高兴) gāoxìng IC1a
plum *n.* 李 lǐ IC1a
polite *adj.* 客氣 (客气) kèqi IC1a
politics *n.* 政治 zhèngzhì IC1b
population *n.* 人口 rénkǒu IC1b
post office *n.* 郵局 (邮局) yóujú IC1b
postcard *n.* 明信片 míngxìnpiàn IC1b
practice *v.* 練習 (练习) liànxí IC1a, 實習 (实习) shíxí L5
prefer *v.* 喜歡 (喜欢) xǐhuan IC1a
prepare *v.* 準備 (准备) zhǔnbèi IC1b
present[1] *v.* 在 zài IC1a
present[2] *n.* 禮物 (礼物) lǐwù IC1b
pressing *adj.* 急 jí IC1b
pretty *adj.* 漂亮 (漂亮) piàoliang IC1a
pretty good *adj.* 不錯 (不错) búcuò IC1a
preview *v.* 預習 (预习) yùxí IC1a
price *n.* 價 (价) jià IC1b
probable *aux.* 會 (会) huì IC1a
problem *n.* 問題 (问题) wèntí IC1a
pronunciation *n.* 發音 (发音) fāyīn IC1a
properly *adv.* 好好 (兒) (好好 [儿)] hǎohāo(r) IC1b
public *adj.* 公共 gōnggòng IC1a
punish *v.* 罰 (罚) fá IC1b
put *v.* 放 fàng IC1b,
~ in *v.* 放 fàng IC1b, 加 jiā IC1b
put in order *v.* 整理 zhěnglǐ IC1b
put on (clothing) *v.* 穿 chuān IC1a

Q

quarter[1] *adv-t.* 刻 kè IC1a,
~ (hour) *adv-t.* 刻 kè IC1a
quarter[2] *n.* 學期 (学期) xuéqī IC1a
question *n.* 問題 (问题) wèntí IC1a
quick *adj.* 快 kuài IC1a
quiet *adj.* 安靜 (安静) ānjìng IC1b
quite a few *adv.* 好幾 (好几) hǎo jǐ IC1b

R

racket *n.* 拍 pāi IC1b
rain *vo.* 下雨 xià yǔ IC1a
raise *v.* 養 (养) yǎng IC1b
read *v.* 看 kàn IC1a, 唸 (念) niàn IC1a,
~ (books) *vo.* 看書 (看书) kànshū IC1a
really *adv.* 真 zhēn IC1a
really hurt *vc.* 疼死 téng sǐ IC1b
recall *vc.* 想起來 (想起来) xiǎng qilai IC1b
receive *v.* 接 jiē IC1b, 受 shòu IC1b, *vc.* 收到 shōu dào IC1b, *vo.* 受傷 (受伤) shòu shāng IC1b
recently *adv-t.* 最近 (最近) zuìjìn IC1a
recognize *v.* 認識 (认识) rènshi IC1a
recording *n.* 錄音 (录音) lùyīn IC1a
red *adj.* 紅 (红) hóng IC1a,
~ leaves *n.* 紅葉 (红叶) hóngyè IC1a
register (mail) *vo.* 掛號 (挂号) guà hào IC1b
regular mail *n.* 平信 píngxìn IC1b
relative, ~s *n.* 親戚 (亲戚) qīnqi IC1b
remain *v.* 剩 shèng IC1b
remember *v.* 記得 (记得) jìde IC1b, *vc.* 想起來 (想起来) xiǎng qilai IC1b
remind *v.* 提醒 tíxǐng IC1b
renew *v.* 續借 (续借) xùjiè IC1b
Renminbi (RMB, Chinese currency) *n.* 人民幣 (人民币) Rénmínbì IC1b
rent *n.* 房租 (房租) fángzū IC1b; *v.* 租 zū IC1b,
~ out 出租 chūzū IC1a
reserve *v.* 訂 (订) dìng IC1b, L9

restaurant *n.* 飯館兒 (饭馆儿) fànguǎnr IC1b
restroom *n.* 廁所 (厕所) cèsuǒ IC1b
return *v.* 回 huí IC1a, *vc.* 回來 (回来) huílai IC1a; *v.* 還 (还) huán IC1b
review *v.* 復習 (复习) fùxí IC1a
rice *n.* 飯 (饭) fàn IC1a
right[1] *adj.* 對 (对) duì IC1a, IC1b
right[2] *n.* 右 yòu IC1b,
~ side *adv-l.* 右邊 (右边) yòubiān IC1b
right away *adv.* 趕快 (赶快) gǎnkuài IC1b
river *n.* 河 hé IC1b
road *n.* 公路 gōnglù IC1a, 路 lù IC1a
room *n.* 房間 (房间) fángjiān IC1b
round *adj.* 圓 (圆) yuán IC1b
round trip *n.* 來回 (来回) láihuí IC1b
run *v.* 跑 pǎo IC1b
run out of *v.* 完 wán IC1b

S

same *adj.* 一樣 (一样) yíyàng IC1a, *adv.* 同 tóng IC1b
say *v.* 說 (说) shuō IC1a
scenery *n.* 風景 (风景) fēngjǐng IC1b
scheduled flight *n.* 班機 (班机) bānjī IC1b
school *n.* 學校 (学校) xuéxiào IC1a
school term *n.* 學期 (学期) xuéqī IC1a
schoolwork *n.* 功課 (功课) gōngkè IC1a
script *n.* 文 wén IC1a
sea *n.* 海 hǎi IC1a
season *n.* 季 jì IC1b
seat *n.* 位子 wèizi IC1b, 座位 zuòwei IC1b
section *n.* 部 (部) bù IC1b
security deposit *n.* 押金 yājīn IC1b
see *v.* 見 (见) jiàn IC1a
see off/out *v.* 送 (送) sòng IC1a
seem *adv.* 好像 (好象) hǎoxiàng IC1b
sell *v.* 賣 (卖) mài IC1b
semester *n.* 學期 (学期) xuéqī IC1a
send by mail *v.* 寄 jì IC1b
sensitive *adj.* 過敏 (过敏) guòmǐn IC1b
serious *adj.* 重 zhòng IC1b
serve as *v.* 當 (当) dāng IC1b
serve dishes *vo.* 上菜 (上菜) shàng cài IC1b
service *n.* 服務 (服务) fúwù IC1b,
~ counter *n.* 服務台 (服务台) fúwùtái IC1b
several months *n.* 幾個月 (几个月) jǐ ge yuè IC1b
she *pron.* 她 tā IC1a
shed *v.* 流 liú IC1b
shirt *n.* 襯衫 (衬衫) chènshān IC1a
shoe(s) *n.* 鞋 xié IC1a
shop *n.* 店 (店) diàn IC1b
shop assistant *n.* 售貨員 (售货员) shòuhuòyuán IC1a
should *adv.* 應該 (应该) yīnggāi IC1b
show (a film) *v.* 演 yǎn IC1b
shower *v.* 洗澡 xǐzǎo IC1a
shut *v.* 閉 (闭) bì IC1b
side *n.* 邊 (边) biān IC1b, 旁邊 (旁边) pángbiān IC1b
simple *adj.* 簡單 (简单) jiǎndān IC1b
sing *v.* 唱 chàng IC1a,
~ a song *vo.* 唱歌 chàng gē IC1a
single *n.* 單 (单) dān IC1b,
~ bed *n.* 單人床 (单人床) dānrénchuáng IC1b
sit *v.* 坐 zuò IC1a
size *n.* 大小 dàxiǎo IC1a, 號 (号) hào IC1a
ski (snow) *vo.* 滑雪 huá xuě IC1b
sleep *v.* 睡 shuì IC1a, *vo.* 睡覺 (睡觉) shuì jiào IC1a
slide *v.* 滑 huá IC1b
slow *adj.* 慢 màn IC1a
small *adj.* 小 xiǎo IC1a
smart *adj.* 帥 (帅) shuài IC1a
snow *n.* 雪 xuě IC1b
so[1] *conj.* 所以 suǒyǐ IC1a
so[2] *pron.* 這麼 (这么) zhème IC1a, 這樣 (这样) zhèyàng IC1a
soccer *n.* 足球 zúqiú IC1b
sofa *n.* 沙發 (沙发) shāfā IC1b
soft drink *n.* 汽水 (汽水) qìshuǐ IC1b
sold out *vc.* 賣完 (了) [卖完 (了)] mài wán (le) IC1b
some[1] *num.* 幾 (几) jǐ IC1a
some[2] *adv.* 點兒 (点儿) diǎnr IC1a,
ph. 有一點兒 (有一点儿) yǒu yìdiǎnr IC1a;
adv. 一些 yìxiē IC1b; 有的 yǒude IC1b
sometimes *ph.* 有時候 (有时候) yǒu shíhou IC1a
somewhat *ph* 有一點兒 (有一点儿) yǒu yìdiǎnr IC1a
son *n.* 兒子 (儿子) érzi IC1a
song *n.* 歌 gē IC1a
soon *adv* 快 kuài IC1a
sorry *ph.* 對不起 (对不起) duìbuqǐ IC1a
sound *n.* 聲音 (声音) shēngyīn L13,
~ recording *n.* 錄音 (录音) lùyīn IC1a
sound like *vc.* 聽起來 (听起来) tīng qilai IC1b

soup *n.* 湯 (汤) tāng IC1b
sour *adj.* 酸 suān IC1b
south *n.* 南 nán IC1b
speak *v.* 說 (说) shuō IC1a, *vo.* 說話 (说话) shuō huà IC1a
special *adj.* 特別 tèbié IC1b
specialty *n.* 專業 (专业) zhuānyè IC1a
speech *n.* 話 (话) huà IC1a
spend *v.* 費 (费) fèi IC1b, *v.* 花 (花) huā IC1a,
~ money *vo.* 花錢 (花钱) huā qián IC1b
sports *n.* 運動 (运动) yùndòng IC1b,
~ field *n.* 運動場 (运动场) yùndòngchǎng IC1b,
~wear *n.* 運動服 (运动服) yùndòngfú IC1b
spring *n.* 春天 chūntiān IC1a
spring break *n.* 春假 chūnjià IC1b
staff member *n.* 職員 (职员) zhíyuán IC1b
stamp *n.* 郵票 (邮票) yóupiào IC1b
start *v.* 開始 (开始) kāishǐ IC1a
starve *v.* 餓 (饿) è IC1b,
~ to death *vc.* 餓死 (饿死) è sǐ IC1b
station *n.* (車) 站 [(车) 站] (chē)zhàn IC1a
stomach *n.* 肚子 dùzi IC1b
stop[1] *n.* [(車) 站 [(车) 站] (chē)zhàn IC1a
stop[2] *v.* 停 tíng IC1b
store *n.* 店 (店) diàn IC1b
straight *adv.* 一直 yìzhí IC1b
strength *n.* 力氣 (力气) lìqi IC1b
student *n.* 學生 (学生) xuésheng IC1a,
~ ID *n.* 學生證 (学生证) xuéshēngzhèng IC1b,
~ studying abroad *n.* 留學生 (留学生) liúxuéshēng IC1b
studious *adj.* 用功 yònggōng IC1b
study *v.* 看書 (看书) kàn shū IC1a, 學 (学) xué IC1a
stuff *n.* 東西 (东西) dōngxi IC1a
stuffy *adj.* 悶 (闷) mēn IC1a
subjected to *vo./adj.* 受傷 (受伤) shòu shāng IC1b
subscribe to *v.* 訂 (订) dìng IC1b
subway *n.* 地鐵 (地铁) dìtiě IC1a
such *pron.* 這麼 (这么) zhème IC1a
suffer *vo.* 受傷 (受伤) shòu shāng IC1b
sugar *n.* 糖 táng IC1b
suitable *adj.* 合適 (合适) héshì IC1a
summer *n.* 夏天 xiàtiān IC1a,
~ school *n.* 署期學校 (署期学校) shǔqī xuéxiào IC1b,
~ vacation *n.* 暑假 shǔjià IC1b, L1
sun *n.* 日 rì IC1a
superhighway *n.* 高速公路 (高速公路) gāosù gōnglù IC1a
supper *n.* 晚飯 (晚饭) wǎnfàn IC1a
surname *n.* 姓 xìng IC1a
sweep *v.* 掃 (扫) sǎo IC1b
sweet *adj.* 甜 tián IC1b
swim *v.* 游泳 yóuyǒng IC1b

T

table *n.* 桌子 zhuōzi IC1b
take *v.* 拿 ná IC1b
take (effort) *v.* 費 (费) fèi IC1b
take a test/exam *v.* 考 kǎo IC1a, *vo.* 考試 (考试) kǎo shì IC1a
take after *v.* 像 (象) xiàng IC1b
take care (of oneself) *v.* 保重 bǎozhòng IC1b
take off *v.* 起飛 (起飞) qǐfēi IC1b
take part in *v.* 參加 (参加) cānjiā IC1b
take someone somewhere *v.* 送 (送) sòng IC1a
talk *n.* 話 (话) huà IC1a, *vo.* 說話 (说话) shuō huà IC1a,
~ about *vc.* 說到 (说到) shuō dào IC1b
tall *adj.* 高 gāo IC1a, IC1b
taxi *n.* 出租汽車 (出租汽车) chūzū qìchē IC1a
tea *n.* 茶 (茶) chá IC1a
teach *v.* 教 jiāo IC1a
teacher *n.* 老師 (老师) lǎoshī IC1a
tear *n.* 眼淚 (眼泪) yǎnlèi IC1b
telephone *n.* 電話 (电话) diànhuà IC1a
tell *v.* 告訴 (告诉) gàosu IC1a
tennis *n.* 網球 (网球) wǎngqiú IC1b
terrible mess *adj.* 糟糕 zāogāo IC1a
test *n.* 考試 (考试) kǎoshì IC1a, *vo.* 考試 (考试) kǎo shì IC1a
text *n.* 課文 (课文) kèwén IC1a
thank you *ph.* 謝謝 (谢谢) xièxie IC1a
thanks *n.* 謝 (谢) Xiè IC1a
that *pron.* 那 (那) nà / nèi IC1a
then *conj.* 那 (那) nà IC1a, 那麼 (那么) nàme IC1b; *adv./conj.* 然後 (然后) ránhòu IC1a
then (sooner than expected) *adv.* 就 jiù IC1a
then and only then *adv.* 再 zài IC1b
there *pron.* 那兒 (那儿) nàr IC1a, 那裡 (那里) nàlǐ IC1b
these *pron.* 這些 (这些) zhè(i)xiē IC1b
thin *adj.* 瘦 shòu IC1b
things *n.* 東西 (东西) dōngxi IC1a

think *v.* 想 xiǎng IC1a;
~ erroneously (wrongly) *v.* 以為 (以为) yǐwéi IC1b
thirsty *adj.* 渴 kě IC1b
this *pron.* 這 (这) zhè / zhèi IC1a, 這個 (这个) zhè(i)ge IC1a
this year *adv-t.* 今年 jīnnián IC1a
thousand *num.* 千 qiān IC1b
ticket *n.* 票 piào IC1a
tidy up *v.* 收拾 shōushi IC1b
time *n.* 次 cì IC1a, 時候 (时候) shíhou IC1a; *adv-t.* 時間 (时间) shíjiān IC1a
tired *adj.* 累 lèi IC1b
to *prep.* 給 (给) gěi IC1a
today *adv-t.* 今 jīn IC1a, 今天 jīntiān IC1a
tofu *n.* 豆腐 dòufu IC1b
together *adv.* 一起 yìqǐ IC1a
toilet *n.* 廁所 (厕所) cèsuǒ IC1b
toilsome *adj.* 辛苦 (辛苦) xīnkǔ IC1b
tomorrow *adv-t.* 明天 míngtiān IC1a, *n.* 明兒 (明儿) míngr IC1b
too *adv.* 也 yě IC1a
tour guide *n.* 導遊 (导遊) dǎoyóu IC1b
toward(s) *prep.* 往 wàng/wǎng IC1b
town *n.* 城 chéng IC1b, 鎮 (镇) zhèn IC1b
traffic light *n.* 紅綠燈 (红绿灯) hónglǜdēng IC1b
travel *v.* 旅行 lǚxíng IC1b,
~ agency *n.* 旅行社 lǚxíngshè IC1b
travel by *v.* 坐 zuò IC1a
treat *v.* 請 (请) qǐng IC1a
troublesome *adj.* 麻煩 (麻烦) máfan IC1a
trustworthiness *n.* 信用 xìnyòng IC1b
try *v.* 試 (试) shì IC1b
turn *v.* 拐 (拐) guǎi IC1b
turn into *v.* 成 chéng IC1b
TV *n.* 電視 (电视) diànshì IC1a
two *n.* 兩 (两) liǎng IC1a,
~ (people) *nm. coll.* 倆 (俩) liǎ IC1b

U

U.S. currency *n.* 美元 Měiyuán IC1b
unable to tell *vc.* 看不出來 (看不出来) kàn bu chulai IC1b
unable to find *vc.* 找不到 zhǎo bu dào IC1b
uncle *n.* 伯伯 bóbo IC1b
uncomfortable *adj.* 難受 (难受) nánshòu IC1b
understand *v.* 懂 (懂) dǒng IC1a
university *n.* 大學 (大学) dàxué IC1a,
~ student *n.* 大學生 (大学生) dàxuéshēng IC1a
urgent *adj.* 急 jí IC1b
use *v.* 用 yòng IC1a
used to *v.* 慣 (惯) guàn IC1b
usually *adv.* 平常 píngcháng IC1a

V

vacation *n.* 假 jià IC1b
vegetarian *adj.* 素 sù IC1b
vehicle *n.* 車 (车) chē IC1a, 汽車 (汽车) qìchē IC1a
very *adv.* 很 hěn IC1a, 非常 (非常) fēicháng IC1b
video recording *n.* 錄像 (录像) lùxiàng IC1a
vinegar *n.* 醋 cù IC1b
virtue *n.* 德 dé IC1b
visa *n.* 簽證 (签证) qiānzhèng IC1b
visit relatives *vo.* 探親 (探亲) tàn qīn IC1b

W

wait *v.* 等 děng IC1a
waiter *n.* 服務員 (服务员) fúwùyuán IC1b
walk *v.* 走 zǒu IC1a, *vo.* 走路 zǒu lù IC1b, 行 xíng IC1b
want *v.* 想 xiǎng IC1a, 要 yào IC1a
warm (weather) *adj.* 暖和 nuǎnhuo IC1a
watch *v.* 看 kàn IC1a
water *n.* 水 shuǐ IC1a,
~ and electricity *n.* 水電 (水电) shuǐdiàn IC1b
way (of doing something) *n.* 辦法 (办法) bànfǎ IC1b
we *pron.* 我們 (我们) wǒmen IC1a
wear *v.* 穿 chuān IC1a
weather *n.* 天氣 (天气) tiānqì IC1a, 氣候 (气候) qìhòu IC1b
wee hours *adv-t.* 半夜 bànyè IC1a
week *n.* 星期 xīngqī IC1a;
last ~ *adv-t.* 上個星期 (上个星期) shàngge xīngqī IC1a,
next ~ *adv-t.* 下個星期 (下个星期) xiàge xīngqi IC1a
weekend *adv-t.* 週末 (周末) zhōumò IC1a
welcome *v.* 歡迎 (欢迎) huānyíng IC1b
well *conj.* 那 (那) nà IC1a
west *n.* 西 xī IC1b,
~ side *n.* 西邊 (西边) xībian IC1b
Western food *n.* 西餐 Xīcān IC1b

what *quest. pron.* 什麼 (什么) shénme IC1a
where *quest. pron.* 哪兒 (哪儿) nǎr IC1a, 哪裡 (哪里) nǎli IC1b
which *quest. pron.* 哪 (哪) nǎ / něi IC1a
white *adj.* 白 bái IC1a
who *quest. pron.* 誰 (谁) shéi IC1a
whole family *n.* 一家 yìjiā IC1b
why *quest. pron.* 為什麼 (为什么) wèishénme IC1a
will *aux.* 要 yào IC1a
willing *aux.* 願意 (愿意) yuànyì IC1b
win (a game, etc.) *v.* 贏 (赢) yíng IC1b
wind *n.* 風 (风) fēng IC1b
wine *n.* 酒 jiǔ IC1a
winter *n.* 冬天 dōngtiān IC1a,
~ vacation *n.* 寒假 hánjià IC1a
wish *v.* 祝 zhù IC1a
with *conj.* 跟 gēn IC1a
within *n.* 內 nèi IC1b
without *adv.* 沒 (没) méi IC1a
word *n.* 字 zì IC1a
words *n.* 話 (话) huà IC1a
work *v.* 工作 gōngzuò IC1a
worry *v.* 擔心 (担心) dānxīn IC1b
wound *n.* 傷 (伤) shāng IC1b
write *v.* 寫 (写) xiě IC1a
written language *n.* 文 wén IC1a
wrong *adj.* 錯 (错) cuò IC1a, IC1b

Y

year *n.* 年 nián IC1a, 歲 (岁) suì IC1a,
~ before last *adv-t.* 前年 qiánnián IC1b
yellow *n.* 黃 (黄) huáng IC1a
yesterday *adv-t.* 昨天 zuótiān IC1a
you *pron.* 你 nǐ IC1a,
~ (polite) *pron.* 您 nín IC1a
young *adj.* 年輕 (年轻) shǎo IC1a
younger sister *n.* 妹妹 mèimei IC1a,
~ brother *n.* 弟弟 dìdi IC1a
yuan (unit of Chn currency) *n.* 元 yuán IC1b

TRADITIONAL CHINESE RADICAL INDEX

214 Radicals Arranged by Stroke Count

(Sometimes this is the first step in finding a character in the following Character Index.)

1 筆畫

1	一		one
2	丨		rod
3	丶		dot
4	丿		bent
5	乙		bent
6	亅		downstroke

2 筆畫

7	二		two
8	亠		lid
9	人	亻	man
10	儿		legs
11	入		enter
12	八		eight
13	冂		borders
14	冖		cover
15	冫		ice
16	几		stool
17	凵		pit
18	刀	刂	knife
19	力		power
20	勹		wrap
21	匕		spoon
22	匚		basket
23	匸		box
24	十		ten
25	卜		divination
26	卩		seal
27	厂		cliff
28	厶		cocoon
29	又		hand

3 筆畫

30	口		mouth
31	囗		enclosure
32	土		earth
33	士		scholar
34	夂		pursue
35	夊		persevere
36	夕		dusk
37	大		big
38	女		woman
39	子		child
40	宀		roof
41	寸		inch
42	小		small
43	尢		lame
44	尸		corpse
45	屮		sprout
46	山		mountain
47	川	巛	river
48	工		labor
49	己		self
50	巾		cloth
51	干		pestle
52	幺		tiny
53	广		shelter
54	廴		move on
55	廾		fold hands
56	弋		dart
57	弓		bow
58	彐		pig's snout
59	彡		stripes
60	彳		footstep

4 筆畫

61	心	忄	heart
62	戈		halberd
63	戶	户	doorleaf
64	手	扌	hand
65	支		branch
66	攴	攵	tap
67	文		writing
68	斗		peck
69	斤		axe
70	方		square
71	无		not
72	日		sun
73	曰		speech
74	月		moon
75	木		wood
76	欠		breath
77	止		stop
78	歹		decay
79	殳		strike
80	毋		do not
81	比		to compare
82	毛		hair
83	氏		surname
84	气		gas
85	水	氵	water
86	火	灬	fire
87	爪		claw
88	父		father
89	爻		intertwine
90	爿		splitwood-l
91	片		splitwood-r
92	牙		tooth
93	牛		cow
94	犬	犭	dog

5 筆畫

95	玄		obstruse
96	玉	王	jade
97	瓜		melon
98	瓦		tile
99	甘		sweet
100	生		life
101	用		use
102	田		field
103	疋		roll
104	疒		illness
105	癶		both feet
106	白		white
107	皮		skin
108	皿		dish
109	目		eye
110	矛		spear
111	矢		arrow
112	石		stone
113	示		to reveal
114	禸		track
115	禾		grain
116	穴		cave
117	立		to stand

6 筆畫

118	竹		bamboo
119	米		rice
120	糸		silk
121	缶		container
122	网		net
123	羊		sheep
124	羽		wing
125	老		old
126	而		and
127	耒		plow
128	耳		ear
129	聿		stylus
130	肉		flesh
131	臣		official
132	自		self
133	至		to
134	臼		mortar
135	舌		tongue
136	舛		opposition
137	舟		boat
138	艮		defiance
139	色		color
140	艸	艹	grass
141	虍		tiger
142	虫		insect
143	血		blood
144	行		to go
145	衣		clothing
146	西		west

7 筆畫

147	見		to see
148	角		horn
149	言		speech
150	谷		valley
151	豆		bean
152	豕		pig
153	豸		cat
154	貝		cowry
155	赤		red
156	走		to walk

157 足 foot
158 身 body
159 車 vehicle
160 辛 spicy
161 辰 period
162 辵 辶 to move
163 邑 阝 city
164 酉 wine jug
165 釆 footprint
166 里 1/3 mile

8 筆畫

167 金 metal
168 長 long
169 門 door
170 阜 阝 mound
171 隶 seize
172 隹 short-tailed bird
173 雨 rain
174 青 green
175 非 not

9 筆畫

176 面 face
177 革 rawhide
178 韋 leather
179 韭 leek
180 音 sound
181 頁 page
182 風 wind
183 飛 to fly
184 食 to eat
185 首 head
186 香 fragrant

10 筆畫

187 馬 horse
188 骨 bone
189 高 tall
190 髟 hairlocks
191 鬥 fight
192 鬯 container
193 鬲 caldron
194 鬼 ghost

11 筆畫

195 魚 fish
196 鳥 bird
197 鹵 salt
198 鹿 deer
199 麥 wheat
200 麻 hemp
201 黃 yellow

12 筆畫

201 黃 yellow
202 黍 millet
203 黑 black
204 黹 embroidery

13 筆畫

205 黽 turtle
206 鼎 tripod
207 鼓 drum
208 鼠 rat

14 筆畫

209 鼻 nose
210 齊 even

15 筆畫

211 齒 teeth

16 筆畫

212 龍 dragon
213 龜 tortoise

17 筆畫

214 龠 flute

Integrated Chinese I (Parts 1 & 2)
Traditional Chinese Character Index
Arranged by 214 Radicals

(Totaling approximately 740 characters.)

1 一 部

一	yī	Num
七	qī	Num
三	sān	Num
上	shàng	3.1
下	xià	5.1
不	bù	1.2
且	qiě	10.1
兩	liǎng	2.2

2 丨 部

中	zhōng	1.2

3 丶 部

4 丿 部

久	jiǔ	4.2

5 乙 部

九	jiǔ	Num
也	yě	1.2

6 亅 部

了	le	3.1
事	shì	3.2

7 二 部

二	èr	Num
五	wǔ	Num
些	xiē	12.1

8 亠 部

亮	liàng	5.1
京	jīng	14.2

9 人 亻 部

人	rén	1.2
今	jīn	3.1
介	jiè	5.1
什	shén	1.1
以	yǐ	4.1
他	tā	2.1
付	fù	9.1
件	jiàn	9.1
住	zhù	14.1
作	zuò	5.1
你	nǐ	1.1
但	dàn	6.2
伯	bó	22.1
位	wèi	6.1
來	lái	5.1
保	bǎo	16.2
便	biàn	6.1
便	pián	9.1
信	xìn	8.2
倆	liǎ	17.1
俱	jù	18.1
個	gè	2.1
借	jiiè	13.1
候	hòu	4.1
們	men	3.1
停	tíng	23.1
健	jiàn	16.2
假	jià	11.1
傢	jiā	18a
傅	fù	12.2
備	bèi	18a
傷	shāng	20.2
像	xiàng	10.1
價	jià	21.1

10 儿 部

元	yuán	18.2
先	xiān	1.1
兒	ér	2.1

11 入 部

內	nèi	21.2
兩	liǎng	2.2

12 八 部

八	bā	Num
六	liù	Num
公	gōng	6.1
共	gòng	9.1
其	qí	13.1
典	diǎn	13.2

13 冂 部

再	zài	3.1

14 冖 部

15 冫 部

冬	dōng	10.2
冷	lěng	10.2

16 几 部

17 凵 部

出	chū	10.2

18 刀 刂 部

刀	dāo	Rad
分	fēn	9.1
別	bié	4.2
初	chū	21.2
刻	kè	3.2
到	dào	6.1
前	qián	8.1
剛	gāng	10.2
劃	huà	21.1
劇	jù	17.2

19 力 部

力	lì	17.1
加	jiā	17.1
功	gōng	7.2
助	zhù	7.1
務	wù	12.1

20 勹 部

21 匕 部

北	běi	10.2

22 匚 部

23 匸 部

24 十 部

十	shí	Num
千	qiān	21.2
午	wǔ	6.1
半	bàn	3.1
南	nán	14.2
準	zhǔn	18a

25 卜 部

卡	kǎ	13.1

26 卩部

印 yìn 17.1
危 wēi 20.1

27 厂部

28 厶部

去 qù 4.1
參 cān 17.1

29 又部

又 yòu 10.2
友 yǒu 1.1
及 jí 13.1
受 shòu 20.1

30 口部

口 kǒu 14.2
可 kě 3.1
司 sī 21.1
叫 jiào 1.1
右 yòu 14.2
只 zhǐ 4.2
另 lìng 19.1
台 tái 10.2
吃 chī 3.1
合 hé 9.2
同 tóng 3.2
各 gè 21.1
名 míng 1.1
告 gào 8.1
吵 chǎo 18.1
吧 ba 5.1
呀 ya 5.1
咖 kā 5.1
呢 ne 1.1
味 wèi 12.1
和 hé 2.2
哎 āi 14.2
哥 gē 2.2
哭 kū 23.1
員 yuán 9.1
哪 nǎ 5.1
啤 pí 5.1
唱 chàng 4.1
問 wèn 1.1
啊 a 6.2
售 shòu 9.1
啡 fēi 5.1
唸 niàn 7.2
喜 xǐ 3.1
單 dān 14.2
喝 hē 5.1
喂 wèi/wéi 6.1
嗎 ma 1.2
嘴 zuǐ 15.2

31 囗部

囗 wéi Rad
四 sì Num
回 huí 5.2
因 yīn 3.2
國 guó 1.2
園 yuán 10.1
圓 yuán 20.2
圖 tú 5.2

32 土部

土 tǔ Rad
在 zài 3.2
地 dì 11.1
坐 zuò 5.1
城 chéng 14.2
報 bào 8.1
場 chǎng 11.1
塊 kuài 9.1
壞 huài 16.1

33 士部

34 夂部

35 夊部

夏 xià 10.1

36 夕部

夕 xī Rad
外 wài 4.1
多 duō 3.1
夜 yè 7.2
夠 gòu 12.1

37 大部

大 dà 3.1
天 tiān 3.1
太 tài 3.1
套 tào 18a

38 女部

女 nǚ 2.1
奶 nǎi 23.2
她 tā 2.1
如 rú 13.2
好 hǎo 1.1
姐 jiě 1.1
始 shǐ 7.2
妹 mèi 2.1
姆 mǔ 15.2
姓 xìng 1.1
婆 pó 22.1
媽 mā 2.1

39 子部

子 zǐ 2.1
存 cún 19.2
字 zì 1.1
季 jì 22.1
孩 hái 2.1
孫 sūn 23.2
學 xué 1.2

40 宀部

它 tā 19.2
安 ān 18.2
完 wán 12.2
定 dìng 14.1
客 kè 4.1
室 shì 6.1
容 róng 7.1
家 jiā 2.2
宿 sù 8.1
寄 jì 19.1
寒 hán 11.1
實 shí 13.1
寫 xiě 7.1

41 寸部

寸 cùn Rad
封 fēng 8.2
專 zhuān 8.2
將 jiāng 15.2
對 duì 4.1
導 dǎo 22.2

42 小部

小 xiǎo 1.1
少 shǎo 9.1

43 尢部

就 jiù 6.1

44 尸部

局 jú 19.1

45 屮部

46 山部

山 shān 22.1

47 川巛部

州 zhōu 22.1

48 工部

工 gōng 5.1
差 chà 23.1

49 己部

己 jǐ 11.2
已 yǐ 8.1

50 巾部

市 shì 22.1
希 xī 8.2
帥 shuài 7.2
師 shī 1.2
帶 dài 13.1
常 cháng 4.1
幣 bì 19.2
幫 bāng 6.2

51 干部

平 píng 7.2
年 nián 3.1

52 幺部

幺 yāo Rad
幾 jǐ 2.2

53 广部

床 chuáng 8.1
店 diàn 14.1
廁 cè 16.1
座 zuò 22.1
康 kāng 16.2
廣 guǎng 18a
廚 chú 18a
廳 tīng 8.1

54 廴部

55 廾部

56 弋部

57 弓部

弓 gōng Rad
弟 dì 2.1
張 zhāng 2.1
彈 tán 15.2

58 彐部

59 彡部

影 yǐng 4.1

60 彳部

往 wǎng/wàng 14.2
後 hòu 6.1
律 lǜ 2.2
很 hěn 3.2
從 cóng 14.2
得 de/děi 4.2/6.1
復 fù 7.1

61 心忄部

心 xīn 14.1
必 bì 13.2
忙 máng 3.2
忘 wàng 13.1
念 niàn 7.2
快 kuài 9.1
怎 zěn 3.1
急 jí 23.1
思 sī 4.2
您 nín 1.1
悶 mēn 10.2
愛 ài 15.2
想 xiǎng 4.2
意 yì 4.2
慶 qìng 17.2
慢 màn 7.1
慣 guàn 8.2
懂 dǒng 7.1
應 yīng 15.2

62 戈部

戈 gē Rad
成 chéng 17.1
我 wǒ 1.1
或 huò 11.1

63 戶户部

所 suǒ 4.1
房 fáng 17.2

64 手扌部

才 cái 5.2
手 shǒu 20.2
打 dǎ 4.1
托 tuō 23.1
把 bǎ 13.1
找 zhǎo 4.2
抱 bào 20.2
拐 guǎi 14.2
押 yā 18b
拍 pāi 20.1
拿 ná 16.1
指 zhǐ 15.2
掛 guà 19.1
接 jiē 15.1
掃 sǎo 17.2
探 tàn 23.1
換 huàn 9.2
提 tí 20.2
搬 bān 18a
擔 dān 20.2

65 支部

支 zhī 19.2

66 攴攵部

收 shōu 19.2
放 fàng 12.1
政 zhèng 22.2
教 jiāo 7.1
教 jiào 8.1
敏 mǐn 16.2
整 zhěng 17.2

67 文部

文 wén 2.2

68 斗部

69 斤部

斤 jīn 17.1
新 xīn 8.1

70 方部

方 fāng 6.1
旅 lǚ 17.2
旁 páng 14.1

71 无部

72 日部

日 rì 3.1
早 zǎo 7.2
易 yì 7.1
明 míng 3.2
昨 zuó 4.1
春 chūn 10.2

星	xīng	3.1
是	shì	1.2
時	shí	4.1
晚	wǎn	3.1
暖	nuǎn	10.1
暑	shǔ	15.2

73 日部

更	gèng	10.1
書	shū	4.1
最	zuì	8.2
會	huì	6.1

74 月部

月	yuè	3.1
有	yǒu	2.1
服	fú	9.1
朋	péng	1.1
望	wàng	8.2
期	qī	3.1

75 木部

不	bù	1.2
末	mò	4.1
本	běn	13.2
束	shù	19.2
李	lǐ	1.1
杉	shān	21.2
杯	bēi	5.1
東	dōng	9.1
林	lín	15.1
果	guǒ	13.2
架	jià	18b
查	chá	16.1
校	xiào	5.1
桌	zhuō	12.1
條	tiáo	9.1
極	jí	12.2
椅	yǐ	18b
楚	chǔ	8.2
業	yè	8.2
樓	lóu	13.1
樂	lè	5.1
樂	yuè	4.1
樣	yàng	3.1
樹	shù	22.1
機	jī	11.1

76 欠部

次	cì	10.2
歌	gē	4.1
歡	huān	3.1

77 止部

正	zhèng	8.1
步	bù	8.2
歲	suì	3.1

78 歹部

死	sǐ	16.1

79 殳部

80 毋部

母	mǔ	22.1
每	měi	11.2

81 比部

比	bǐ	10.1

82 毛部

毛	máo	9.1

83 氏部

民	mín	19.2

84 气部

氣	qì	6.1

85 水氵部

水	shuǐ	5.1
汁	zhī	15.1
沙	shā	18.2
沒	méi	2.1
汽	qì	11.1
法	fǎ/fà	7.1
治	zhì	22.2
河	hé	22.1
洗	xǐ	8.1
洛	luò	21.2
活	huó	14.1
海	hǎi	10.1
涼	liáng	10.2
淚	lèi	16.2
清	qīng	8.2
港	gǎng	15.2
減	jiǎn	20.1
游	yóu	22.2
渴	kě	12.1
湯	tāng	12.1
準	zhǔn	18a
滑	huá	22.1
演	yǎn	17.1
漲	zhǎng	21.2
漢	hàn	7.1
濟	jì	22.2
灣	wān	10.2

86 火灬部

火	huǒ	Rad
然	rán	9.2
照	zhào	2.1
煩	fán	11.1
熱	rè	10.2
燒	shāo	12.2
燈	dēng	14.2
營	yíng	19.1

87 爪部

為	wéi/wèi	3.2
爲	wéi/wèi	3.2

88 父部

父	fù	22.1
爸	bà	2.1
爺	yé	23.2

89 爻部

90 爿部

91 片部

片	piàn	2.1

92 牙部

93 牛部

牛	niú	12.2
特	tè	20.2

94 犬犭部

狗	gǒu	15.2
猜	cāi	16.2

95 玄部

96 玉王部

王	wáng	1.1
玩	wán	5.2
班	bān	15.1
球	qiú	4.1

現 xiàn 3.2
理 lǐ 17.2
琴 qín 15.2

97 瓜 部

瓜 guā 12.2

98 瓦 部

瓶 píng 5.2

99 甘 部

甜 tián 12.2

100 生 部

生 shēng 1.1

101 用 部

用 yòng 8.2

102 田 部

田 tián 14.1
男 nán 2.1
留 liú 13.1
當 dāng 18b

103 疋 部

104 疒 部

病 bìng 16.1
疼 téng 16.1
癢 yǎng 16.2
瘦 shòu 23.2

105 癶 部

發 fā 8.1

106 白 部

白 bái 3.1
百 bǎi 9.1
的 de 2.1

107 皮 部

皮 pí 23.1

108 皿 部

盛 shèng 21.2
盤 pán 12.1

109 目 部

目 mù Rad
直 zhí 14.2
看 kàn 4.1
真 zhēn 7.2
眼 yǎn 14.2
睛 jīng 14.2
睡 shuì 4.2

110 矛 部

111 矢 部

知 zhī 6.2

112 石 部

碗 wǎn 12.1
碼 mǎ 17.2
磯 jī 21.2

113 示 部

示 shì Rad
社 shè 21.1
祝 zhù 8.2
票 piào 11.1
禮 lǐ 15.2

114 禸 部

115 禾 部

和 hé 2.2
秋 qiū 10.2
租 zū 11.1
程 chéng 21.1
稱 chēng 23.1
種 zhǒng 16.1

116 穴 部

空 kòng/kōng 6.1
穿 chuān 9.1

117 立 部

站 zhàn 11.1

118 竹 部

笑 xiào 8.2
第 dì 7.1
等 děng 6.1
筆 bǐ 7.1
算 suàn 4.1
節 jié 6.1
篇 piān 8.1
箱 xiāng 23.1
簡 jiǎn 20.1
簽 qiān 21.1
籃 lán 20.1

119 米 部

米 mǐ 12.2
糖 táng 12.2
糕 gāo 10.2
糟 zāo 10.2

120 糸 部

糸 mì Rad
約 yuē 10.1
紅 hóng 9.1
紐 niǔ 17.2
素 sù 12.1
級 jí 6.1
紙 zhǐ 18a
紹 shào 5.1
累 lèi 23.2
給 gěi 5.1
經 jīng 8.1
網 wǎng 20.1
綠 lǜ 7.2
緊 jǐn 11.2
練 liàn 6.2
線 xiàn 11.1
續 xù 13.2

121 缶 部

122 网 部

罰 fá 13.2

123 羊 部

美 měi 1.2

124 羽 部

習 xí 6.2

125 老 部

老 lǎo 1.2
考 kǎo 6.1
者 zhě 11.1

126 而 部

而 ér 10.1

127 耒 部

128 耳部

耳 ěr Rad
聊 liáo 5.2
聰 cōng 15.2
職 zhí 13.1
聽 tīng 4.1

129 聿部

130 肉部

肉 ròu 12.1
肚 dù 16.1
胖 pàng 20.1
能 néng 8.2
腐 fǔ 12.1
腳 jiǎo 20.2
腦 nǎo 8.1
腿 tuǐ 15.2

131 臣部

臥 wò 18a

132 自部

自 zì 11.2

133 至部

134 臼部

舊 jiù 22.1
興 xìng 5.1

135 舌部

舍 shè 8.1
舒 shū 10.2

136 舛部

舞 wǔ 4.1

137 舟部

航 háng 21.1

138 艮部

139 色部

色 sè 9.1

140 艸 艹 部

芝 zhī 21.2
花 huā 11.2
苦 kǔ 23.2
英 yīng 2.2
茶 chá 5.1
華 huá 21.1
菜 cài 12.1
葉 yè 10.1
著 zhe 14.2
藥 yào 16.1

141 虍部

號 hào 3.1

142 虫部

143 血部

144 行部

行 xíng/háng 6.1

145 衣部

衣 yī 9.1
表 biǎo 15.1
衫 shān 21.2
被 bèi 20.2
裡 lǐ 7.1
裏 lǐ 7.1
褲 kù 9.1
襯 chèn 9.1

146 西部

西 xī 9.1
要 yào 5.1

147 見部

見 jiàn 3.1
視 shì 4.1
親 qīn 22.1
覺 jiào/jué 4.2

148 角部

149 言部

言 yán 13.1
訂 dìng 19.2
計 jì 21.1
記 jì 8.1
許 xǔ 18.2
詞 cí 7.1
訴 sù 8.1
該 gāi 15.2
試 shì 6.1
話 huà 6.1
說 shuō 6.2
語 yǔ 7.1
認 yǔ 3.2
課 kè 6.1
誰 shéi 2.1
請 qǐng 1.1
謝 xiè 3.1
識 shì 3.2
證 zhèng 13.1
護 hù 21.1
讓 ràng 11.2

150 谷部

151 豆部

豆 dòu 12.1

152 豕部

象 xiàng 17.1

153 豸部

154 貝部

貝 bèi Rad
貨 huò 9.1
貴 guì 1.1
貼 tiē 19.1
費 fèi 17.1
買 mǎi 9.1
賣 mài 12.2
賽 sài 20.2
贏 yíng 20.2

155 赤部

156 走部

走 zǒu 11.1
起 qǐ 5.1
超 chāo 23.1
越 yuè 16.2
趕 gǎn 16.2

157 足部

足 zú 20.2
跑 pǎo 20.1
跳 tiào 4.1
路 lù 11.2
跟 gēn 6.2
踢 tī 20.2

158 身部
身 shēn 16.2
躺 tǎng 16.1

159 車部
車 chē 11.1
輸 shū 20.2
轉 zhuǎn 21.2

160 辛部
辣 là 12.1
辦 bàn 3.1

161 辰部

162 辵 辶 部
迎 yíng 22.1
近 jìn 8.2
送 sòng 11.1
速 sù 11.2
這 zhè 2.1
連 lián 18a
週 zhōu 4.1
進 jìn 5.1
過 guò/guo 11.2
道 dào 6.2
運 yùn 14.1
遠 yuǎn 14.1
還 hái/huán 3.1
邊 biān 8.1

163 邑 阝 部
那 nà 2.1
部 bù 22.2
郵 yóu 19.1
都 dōu 2.2
都 dū 22.2
鄉 xiāng 22.1

164 酉部
酒 jiǔ 5.1
酸 suān 12.1
醋 cù 12.2
醒 xǐng 23.1
醫 yī 2.2

165 釆部

166 里部
里 lǐ 18.1
重 zhòng 16.2

167 金部
金 jīn 14.1
針 zhēn 16.1
銀 yín 19.2
鋼 gāng 15.2
錄 lù 7.2
錢 qián 9.1
錯 cuò 4.2
鎮 zhèn 22.1
鐘 zhōng 3.1
鐵 tiě 11.1

168 長部
長 cháng 15.2
長 zhǎng 15.2

169 門部
門 mén 13.1
閉 bì 14.2
開 kāi 6.1
間 jiān 6.1
悶 mēn 10.2
關 guān 13.1

170 阜 阝 部
阿 ā/a 22.1
除 chú 8.2
險 xiǎn 16.2

171 隶部

172 隹部
隹 zhuī Rad
準 zhǔn 18a
雙 shuāng 9.2
雖 suī 9.2
離 lí 14.1
難 nán 7.1

173 雨部
雨 yǔ 10.1
雪 xuě 22.1
零 líng IC1
電 diàn 4.1

174 青部
靜 jìng 18b

175 非部
非 fēi 18b

176 面部
面 miàn 14.2

177 革部
鞋 xié 9.2

178 韋部
韓 hán 21.2

179 韭部

180 音部
音 yīn 4.1

181 頁部
須 xū 13.2
預 yù 7.1
頭 tóu 13.1
顏 yán 9.1
題 tí 6.1
願 yuàn 20.1

182 風部
風 fēng 22.1

183 飛部
飛 fēi 11.1

184 食部
食 shí Rad
飯 fàn 3.1
餃 jiǎo 12.1
養 yǎng 18b
餓 è 12.1
餐 cān 8.1
館 guǎn 5.2

185 首部
首 shǒu 19.2

186 香部
香 xiāng 21.2

187 馬部
馬 mǎ 16.2
驗 yàn 13.1

188 骨部
體 tǐ 16.2

189 高部

高 gāo 2.1

190 髟部

191 鬥部

192 鬯部

193 鬲部

194 鬼部

195 魚部

魚 yú 12.2
鮮 xiān 19.2

196 鳥部

197 鹵部

198 鹿部

199 麥部

200 麻部

麻 má 11.1
麼 me 1.1

201 黃部

黃 huáng 9.1

202 黍部

203 黑部

黑 hēi 9.2
點 diǎn 3.1

204 黹部

205 黽部

206 鼎部

207 鼓部

208 鼠部

209 鼻部

鼻 bí 15.2

210 齊部

211 齒部

212 龍部

213 龜部

214 龠部

SIMPLIFIED CHINESE RADICAL INDEX

189 Radicals Arranged by Stroke Count

(Sometimes this is the first step in finding a character in the following Character Index.)

1 筆 畫

1	一	one
2	丨	rod
3	丿	bent
4	丶	dot
5	乙	bent

2 筆 畫

6	二	two
7	十	ten
8	厂	cliff
9	匚	box
10	卜	divination
11	刂	vertical knife
12	冂	borders
13	亻	standing man
14	八	eight
15	人	man
16	勹	wrap
17	儿	legs
18	几	stool
19	亠	lid
20	冫	ice
21	冖	cover
22	讠(言)	speech
23	卩	seal
24	阝	mound-l
25	阝	city-r
26	凵	pit
27	刀	knife
28	力	power
29	厶	cocoon
30	又	hand
31	廴	move on

3 筆 畫

32	工	labor
33	土	earth
34	士	scholar
35	艹	grass
36	廾	fold hands
37	大	big
38	尢	lame
39	扌(手)	hand
40	寸	inch
41	弋	dart
42	小	small
43	口	mouth
44	囗	enclosure
45	巾	cloth
46	山	mountain
47	彳	double-man
48	彡	stripes
49	犭	dog
50	夕	dusk
51	夂	pursue
52	饣(食)	food
53	丬	splitwood-l
54	广	shelter
55	门	door
56	氵	3-dot water
57	忄	vertical heart
58	宀	roof
59	辶	to move
60	彐	pig's snout
61	尸	corpse
62	己(巳)	self
63	弓	bow
64	屮	sprout
65	女	woman
66	子	child
67	纟(糸)	silk
68	马	horse
69	幺	tiny
70	巛	river

4 筆 畫

71	王	jade
72	韦	leather
73	木	wood
74	犬	dog
75	歹	decay
76	车	vehicle
77	戈	halberd
78	比	to compare
79	瓦	tile
80	止	stop
81	攴	tap
82	日	sun
83	曰	speak
84	水	water
85	贝	cowry
86	见	to see
87	牛	cow
88	手	hand
89	毛	hair
90	气	gas
91	攵	tap
92	片	splitwood-r
93	斤	axe
94	爪	claw
95	父	father
96	月	moon
97	欠	breath
98	风	wind
99	殳	strike
100	文	writing
101	方	square
102	火	fire
103	斗	peck
104	灬	4-dot fire
105	户	doorleaf
106	礻(示)	reveal
107	心	heart
108	肀	pen
109	毋	do not

5 筆 畫

110	示	to reveal
111	石	stone
112	龙	dragon
113	业	industry
114	目	eye
115	田	field
116	罒	net
117	皿	dish
118	钅(金)	metal
119	矢	arrow
120	禾	grain
121	白	white
122	瓜	melon
123	用	use
124	鸟	bird
125	疒	illness
126	立	to stand
127	穴	cave
128	衤(衣)	clothing
129	疋	roll
130	皮	skin
131	矛	spear

6 筆 畫

132	耒	plow
133	老	old
134	耳	ear
135	臣	official
136	西	west
137	页	page
138	虍	tiger
139	虫	insect
140	缶	container
141	舌	tongue
142	竹	bamboo
143	臼	mortar
144	自	self
145	血	blood
146	舟	boat
147	衣	clothing
148	羊	sheep
149	米	rice
150	艮	defiance
151	羽	wing
152	糸	silk

7 筆 畫

153	麦	wheat
154	走	to walk
155	赤	red
156	豆	bean

157 酉 wine jug
158 辰 period
159 豕 pig
160 卤 salt
161 里 1/3 mile
162 足 foot
163 身 body
164 釆 footprint
165 谷 valley
166 豸 cat
167 角 horn
168 言 speech
169 辛 spicy

8 筆 畫

170 青 green
171 其 its
172 雨 rain
173 齿 teeth
174 黾 turtle
175 隹 short-tailed bird
176 金 metal
177 鱼 fish

9 筆 畫

178 革 rawhide
179 骨 bone
180 鬼 ghost
181 食 eat
182 音 sound

10 筆 畫

183 鬥 fight
184 髟 hairlocks

11 筆 畫

185 麻 hemp
186 鹿 deer

12 筆 畫

187 黑 black

13 筆 畫

188 鼠 rat

14 筆 畫

189 鼻 nose

Integrated Chinese I (Parts 1 & 2)
Simplified Chinese Character Index

Arranged by 189 Radicals

(Totaling approximately 740 characters.)

1 一 部

一	yī	Num
七	qī	Num
三	sān	Num
上	shàng	3.1
下	xià	5.1
才	cái	5.2
天	tiān	3.1
专	zhuān	8.2
开	kāi	6.1
不	bù	1.2
且	qiě	10.1
平	píng	7.2
东	dōng	9.1
再	zài	3.1
而	ér	10.1
更	gèng	10.1
两	liǎng	2.2
来	lái	5.1
事	shì	3.2
面	miàn	14.2

2 丨 部

中	zhōng	1.2
北	běi	10.2
非	fēi	18b

3 丿 部

九	jiǔ	Num
千	qiān	21.2
久	jiǔ	4.2
么	me	1.1
及	jí	13.1
午	wǔ	6.1
长	cháng	15.2
长	zhǎng	15.2
生	shēng	1.1
乐	lè	5.1
乐	yuè	4.1
年	nián	3.1

4 丶 部

为	wéi/wèi	3.2
头	tóu	13.1
州	zhōu	22.1

5 乙 部

了	le	3.1
也	yě	1.2
飞	fēi	11.1
书	shū	4.1
民	mín	19.2
电	diàn	4.1
买	mǎi	9.1

6 二 部

二	èr	Num
五	wǔ	Num
些	xiē	12.1

7 十 部

十	shí	Num
支	zhī	19.2
卖	mài	12.2
南	nán	14.2
华	huá	21.1
直	zhí	14.2
真	zhēn	7.2

8 厂 部

厅	tīng	8.1
厕	cè	16.1
厨	chú	18a

9 匚 部

医	yī	2.2

10 卜 部

卡	kǎ	13.1

11 刂 部

划	huà	21.1
刚	gāng	10.2
别	bié	4.2
到	dào	6.1
刻	kè	3.2
前	qián	8.1
剧	jù	17.2

12 冂 部

内	nèi	21.2
同	tóng	3.2
网	wǎng	20.1
肉	ròu	12.1
周	zhōu	4.1

13 亻 部

什	shén	1.1
付	fù	9.1
们	men	3.1
他	tā	2.1
件	jiàn	9.1
伤	shāng	20.2
价	jià	21.1
体	tǐ	16.2
但	dàn	6.2
作	zuò	5.1
伯	bó	22.1
你	nǐ	1.1
住	zhù	14.1
位	wèi	6.1
便	biàn	6.1
便	pián	9.1
俩	liǎ	17.1
保	bǎo	16.2
信	xìn	8.2
借	jiiè	13.1
候	hòu	4.1
健	jiàn	16.2
停	tíng	23.1
假	jià	11.1
傅	fù	12.2
像	xiàng	10.1

14 八 部

八	bā	Num
公	gōng	6.1
半	bàn	3.1
关	guān	13.1
共	gòng	9.1
兴	xìng	5.1
弟	dì	2.1
具	jù	18.1
单	dān	14.2
典	diǎn	13.2
首	shǒu	19.2
黄	huáng	9.1

15 人 部

人	rén	1.2
个	gè	2.1
介	jiè	5.1
从	cóng	14.2
今	jīn	3.1
以	yǐ	4.1
会	huì	6.1

16 勹 部

够	gòu	12.1

17 儿部

儿	ér	2.1
元	yuán	18.2
先	xiān	1.1

18 几部

几	jǐ	2.2

19 亠部

六	liù	Num
京	jīng	14.2
夜	yè	7.2
亮	liàng	5.1
高	gāo	2.1
离	lí	14.1
就	jiù	6.1
赢	yíng	20.2

20 冫部

习	xí	6.2
冷	lěng	10.2
准	zhǔn	18a
凉	liáng	10.2
减	jiǎn	20.1

21 冖部

写	xiě	7.1

22 讠部

计	jì	21.1
订	dìng	19.2
认	rèn	3.2
让	ràng	11.2
记	jì	8.1
许	xǔ	18.2
证	zhèng	13.1
识	shì	3.2
诉	sù	8.1
词	cí	7.1
试	shì	6.1
话	huà	6.1
该	gāi	15.2
语	yǔ	7.1
说	shuō	6.2
请	qǐng	1.1
课	kè	6.1
谁	shéi	2.1
谢	xiè	3.1

23 卩部

印	yìn	17.1
危	wēi	20.1

24 阝部

阿	ā/a	22.1
除	chú	8.2
险	xiǎn	16.2

25 阝部

那	nà	2.1
邮	yóu	19.1
都	dōu	2.2
都	dū	22.2
部	bù	22.2

26 凵部

出	chū	10.2

18 刀 刂部

刀	dāo	Rad
分	fēn	9.1
色	sè	9.1
初	chū	21.2

19 力部

力	lì	17.1
办	bàn	3.1
功	gōng	7.2
加	jiā	17.1
务	wù	12.1
助	zhù	7.1

29 厶部

去	qù	4.1
参	cān	17.1

30 又部

又	yòu	10.2
友	yǒu	1.1
双	shuāng	9.2
发	fā	8.1
受	shòu	20.1

31 廴部

32 工部

工	gōng	5.1
差	chà	23.1

33 土部

土	tǔ	Rad
在	zài	3.2
地	dì	11.1
场	chǎng	11.1
坏	huài	16.1
坐	zuò	5.1
块	kuài	9.1
城	chéng	14.2

34 士部

35 艹部

节	jié	6.1
芝	zhī	21.2
花	huā	11.2
苦	kǔ	23.2
英	yīng	2.2
茶	chá	5.1
药	yào	16.1
菜	cài	12.1
营	yíng	19.1

36 廾部

37 大部

大	dà	3.1
太	tài	3.1
套	tào	18a

38 尢部

39 扌部

打	dǎ	4.1
托	tuō	23.1
扫	sǎo	17.2
找	zhǎo	4.2
护	hù	21.1
把	bǎ	13.1
报	bào	8.1
担	dān	20.2
押	yā	18b
拐	guǎi	14.2
拍	pāi	20.1
抱	bào	20.2
挂	guà	19.1
指	zhǐ	15.2
换	huàn	9.2

接 jiē 15.1
探 tàn 23.1
提 tí 20.2
搬 bān 18a

40 寸 部

寸 cùn Rad
对 duì 4.1
导 dǎo 22.2
封 fēng 8.2
将 jiāng 15.2

41 弋 部

42 小 部

小 xiǎo 1.1
少 shǎo 9.1

43 口 部

口 kǒu 14.2
叶 yè 10.1
右 yòu 14.2
可 kě 3.1
号 hào 3.1
只 zhǐ 4.2
司 sī 21.1
叫 jiào 1.1
另 lìng 19.1
台 tái 10.2
吃 chī 3.1
后 hòu 6.1
合 hé 9.2
名 míng 1.1
各 gè 21.1
吗 ma 1.2
呀 ya 5.1
吵 chǎo 18.1
员 yuán 9.1
告 gào 8.1
听 tīng 4.1
吧 ba 5.1
味 wèi 12.1
哎 āi 14.2
和 hé 2.2
呢 ne 1.1
咖 kā 5.1
虽 suī 9.2
哪 nǎ 5.1
哥 gē 2.2
哭 kū 23.1
啊 a 6.2
啡 fēi 5.1
唱 chàng 4.1
售 shòu 9.1
啤 pí 5.1
喜 xǐ 3.1
喝 hē 5.1
喂 wèi/wéi 6.1
嘴 zuǐ 15.2

44 囗 部

囗 wéi Rad
四 sì Num
因 yīn 3.2
回 huí 5.2
园 yuán 10.1
国 guó 1.2
图 tú 5.2
圆 yuán 20.2

45 巾 部

币 bì 19.2
帅 shuài 7.2
市 shì 22.1
师 shī 1.2
希 xī 8.2
帮 bāng 6.2
带 dài 13.1
常 cháng 4.1

46 山 部

山 shān 22.1
岁 suì 3.1

47 彳 部

行 xíng/háng 6.1
往 wǎng/wàng 14.2
律 lǜ 2.2
很 hěn 3.2
得 dé/de 4.2/7.1
得 děi 6.1

48 彡 部

影 yǐng 4.1

49 犭 部

狗 gǒu 15.2
猜 cāi 16.2

50 夕 部

夕 xī Rad
外 wài 4.1
多 duō 3.1

51 夂 攵 部

冬 dōng 10.2
复 fù 7.1
夏 xià 10.1

52 饣 部

饭 fàn 3.1
饺 jiǎo 12.1
饿 è 12.1
馆 guǎn 5.2

53 丬 部

54 广 部

广 guǎng 18a
庆 qìng 17.2
床 chuáng 8.1
应 yīng 15.2
店 diàn 14.1
康 kāng 16.2
腐 fǔ 12.1

55 门 部

门 mén 13.1
闭 bì 14.2
问 wèn 1.1
间 jiān 6.1
闷 mēn 10.2

56 氵 部

汁 zhī 15.1
汉 hàn 7.1
汤 tāng 12.1
沙 shā 18.2
汽 qì 11.1
没 méi 2.1
法 fǎ/fà 7.1
河 hé 22.1
泪 lèi 16.2
治 zhì 22.2
洗 xǐ 8.1
活 huó 14.1
洛 luò 21.2
济 jì 22.2
海 hǎi 10.1

涨 zhǎng 21.2
清 qīng 8.2
港 gǎng 15.2
渴 kě 12.1
滑 huá 22.1
湾 wān 10.2
游 yóu 22.2
演 yǎn 17.1

57 忄 部

忙 máng 3.2
快 kuài 9.1
惯 guàn 8.2
慢 màn 7.1
懂 dǒng 7.1

58 宀 部

它 tā 19.2
安 ān 18.2
字 zì 1.1
完 wán 12.2
定 dìng 14.1
实 shí 13.1
室 shì 6.1
客 kè 4.1
家 jiā 2.2
寄 jì 19.1
宿 sù 8.1
寒 hán 11.1

59 辶 部

边 biān 8.1
过 guò/guo 11.2
进 jìn 5.1
远 yuǎn 14.1
运 yùn 14.1
还 hái 3.1
还 huán 13.1
连 lián 18a
近 jìn 8.2
迎 yíng 22.1
这 zhè 2.1
送 sòng 11.1
速 sù 11.2
道 dào 6.2

60 彐 部

当 dāng 18b

61 尸 部

局 jú 19.1

62 己 部

己 jǐ 11.2
已 yǐ 8.1

63 弓 部

弓 gōng Rad
张 zhāng 2.1
弹 tán 15.2

64 屮 部

65 女 部

女 nǚ 2.1
奶 nǎi 23.2
如 rú 13.2
她 tā 2.1
好 hǎo 1.1
妈 mā 2.1
妹 mèi 2.1
姐 jiě 1.1
姓 xìng 1.1
始 shǐ 7.2
姆 mǔ 15.2
婆 pó 22.1

66 子 部

子 zǐ 2.1
存 cún 19.2
孙 sūn 23.2
学 xué 1.2
孩 hái 2.1

67 纟 部

红 hóng 9.1
约 yuē 10.1
级 jí 6.1
纸 zhǐ 18a
纽 niǔ 17.2
线 xiàn 11.1
练 liàn 6.2
绍 shào 5.1
经 jīng 8.1
给 gěi 5.1
续 xù 13.2
绿 lǜ 7.2

68 马 部

马 mǎ 16.2
验 yàn 13.1

69 幺 部

幺 yāo Rad
乡 xiāng 22.1

70 巛 部

71 王 部

王 wáng 1.1
玩 wán 5.2
现 xiàn 3.2
班 bān 15.1
球 qiú 4.1
理 lǐ 17.2
琴 qín 15.2

72 韦 部

韩 hán 21.2

73 木 部

木 mù Rad
本 běn 13.2
末 mò 4.1
机 jī 11.1
束 shù 19.2
杉 shān 21.2
条 tiáo 9.1
极 jí 12.2
李 lǐ 1.1
林 lín 15.1
杯 bēi 5.1
果 guǒ 13.2
查 chá 16.1
亲 qīn 22.1
架 jià 18b
树 shù 22.1
桌 zhuō 12.1
校 xiào 5.1
样 yàng 3.1
椅 yǐ 18b
楚 chǔ 8.2
楼 lóu 13.1

74 犬 部

75 歹 部

死 sǐ 16.1

76 车 部

车 chē 11.1
转 zhuǎn 21.2
输 shū 20.2

77 戈 部

戈 gē Rad
成 chéng 17.1
我 wǒ 1.1
或 huò 11.1

78 比 部

比 bǐ 10.1

79 瓦 部

瓶 píng 5.2

80 止 部

正 zhèng 8.1
步 bù 8.2

81 支 部

82 日 部

日 rì 3.1
旧 jiù 22.1
早 zǎo 7.2
时 shí 4.1
明 míng 3.2
易 yì 7.1
春 chūn 10.2
是 shì 1.2
星 xīng 3.1
昨 zuó 4.1
晚 wǎn 3.1
暑 shǔ 15.2
暖 nuǎn 10.1

83 日 部

者 zhě 11.1
最 zuì 8.2

84 水 部

水 shuǐ 5.1
录 lù 7.2

85 贝 部

贝 bèi Rad
货 huò 9.1
贴 tiē 19.1
贵 guì 1.1
费 fèi 17.1
赛 sài 20.2

86 见 部

见 jiàn 3.1
视 shì 4.1
觉 jiào/jué 4.2

87 牛 部

牛 niú 12.2
特 tè 20.2

88 手 部

手 shǒu 20.2
拿 ná 16.1

89 毛 部

毛 máo 9.1

90 气 部

气 qì 6.1

91 攵 部

收 shōu 19.2
放 fàng 12.1
政 zhèng 22.2
教 jiāo 7.1
教 jiào 8.1
敏 mǐn 16.2
整 zhěng 17.2

92 片 部

片 piàn 2.1

93 斤 部

斤 jīn 17.1
新 xīn 8.1

94 爪 部

爱 ài 15.2

95 父 部

父 fù 22.1
爷 yé 23.2
爸 bà 2.1

96 月 部

月 yuè 3.1
有 yǒu 2.1
肚 dù 16.1
朋 péng 1.1
服 fú 9.1
胖 pàng 20.1
脑 nǎo 8.1
能 néng 8.2
脚 jiǎo 20.2
望 wàng 8.2
期 qī 3.1
腿 tuǐ 15.2

97 欠 部

次 cì 10.2
欢 huān 3.1
歌 gē 4.1

98 风 部

风 fēng 22.1

99 殳 部

100 文 部

文 wén 2.2

101 方 部

方 fāng 6.1
旅 lǚ 17.2
旁 páng 14.1

102 火 部

火 huǒ Rad
灯 dēng 14.2
烦 fán 11.1
烧 shāo 12.2

103 斗 部

104 灬 部

点 diǎn 3.1
热 rè 10.2

然 rán 9.2
照 zhào 2.1

105 户部

所 suǒ 4.1
房 fáng 17.2

106 衤部

礼 lǐ 15.2
社 shè 21.1
祝 zhù 8.2

107 心部

心 xīn 14.1
必 bì 13.2
忘 wàng 13.1
念 niàn 7.2
思 sī 4.2
怎 zěn 3.1
急 jí 23.1
您 nín 1.1
想 xiǎng 4.2
意 yì 4.2
愿 yuàn 20.1

108 聿部

109 毋部

母 mǔ 22.1
每 měi 11.2

110 示部

示 shì Rad
票 piào 11.1

111 石部

矶 jī 21.2
码 mǎ 17.2
碗 wǎn 12.1

112 龙部

113 业部

业 yè 8.2

114 目部

目 mù Rad
看 kàn 4.1
眼 yǎn 14.2
睛 jīng 14.2
睡 shuì 4.2

115 田部

田 tián 14.1
男 nán 2.1
备 bèi 18a
留 liú 13.1

116 罒部

罚 fá 13.2

117 皿部

盛 shèng 21.2
盘 pán 12.1

118 钅部

针 zhēn 16.1
钟 zhōng 3.1
钢 gāng 15.2
钱 qián 9.1
铁 tiě 11.1
银 yín 19.2
错 cuò 4.2
镇 zhèn 22.1

119 矢部

知 zhī 6.2

120 禾部

和 hé 2.2
季 jì 22.1
香 xiāng 21.2
种 zhǒng 16.1
秋 qiū 10.2
租 zū 11.1
称 chēng 23.1
程 chéng 21.1

121 白部

白 bái 3.1
百 bǎi 9.1
的 de 2.1

122 瓜部

瓜 guā 12.2

123 用部

用 yòng 8.2

124 鸟部

125 疒部

病 bìng 16.1
疼 téng 16.1
痒 yǎng 16.2
瘦 shòu 23.2

126 立部

站 zhàn 11.1

127 穴部

空 kòng/kōng 6.1
穿 chuān 9.1
容 róng 7.1

128 衤部

衬 chèn 9.1
衫 shān 21.2
被 bèi 20.2
裤 kù 9.1

129 疋部

130 皮部

皮 pí 23.1

131 矛部

132 耒部

133 老部

老 lǎo 1.2
考 kǎo 6.1

134 耳部

耳 ěr Rad
职 zhí 13.1
聊 liáo 5.2
聪 cōng 15.2

135 臣 部

卧 wò 18a

136 西 部

西 xī 9.1
要 yào 5.1

137 页 部

须 xū 13.2
预 yù 7.1
题 tí 6.1
颜 yán 9.1

138 虍 部

139 虫 部

140 缶 部

141 舌 部

舍 shè 8.1
甜 tián 12.2
舒 shū 10.2

142 竹 部

笔 bǐ 7.1
笑 xiào 8.2
第 dì 7.1
等 děng 6.1
签 qiān 21.1
简 jiǎn 20.1
筷 kuài
算 suàn 4.1
箱 xiāng 23.1
篇 piān 8.1
篮 lán 20.1

143 臼 部

144 自 部

自 zì 11.2

145 血 部

146 舟 部

航 háng 21.1

147 衣 部

衣 yī 9.1
表 biǎo 15.1

148 羊 部

美 měi 1.2
养 yǎng 18b
着 zhe 14.2

149 米 部

米 mǐ 12.2
糖 táng 12.2
糕 gāo 10.2
糟 zāo 10.2

150 艮 部

151 羽 部

152 糸 部

糸 mì Rad
素 sù 12.1
紧 jǐn 11.2
累 lèi 23.2

153 麦 部

154 走 部

走 zǒu 11.1
赶 gǎn 16.2
起 qǐ 5.1
越 yuè 16.2
超 chāo 23.1

155 赤 部

156 豆 部

豆 dòu 12.1

157 酉 部

酒 jiǔ 5.1
酸 suān 12.1
醋 cù 12.2
醒 xǐng 23.1

158 辰 部

159 豕 部

象 xiàng 17.1

160 卤 部

161 里 部

里 lǐ 7.1
里 lǐ 18.1
重 zhòng 16.2

162 足 部

足 zú 20.2
跑 pǎo 20.1
跳 tiào 4.1
路 lù 11.2
跟 gēn 6.2
踢 tī 20.2

163 身 部

身 shēn 16.2
躺 tǎng 16.1

164 采 部

165 谷 部

166 豸 部

167 角 部

168 言 部

言 yán 13.1

169 辛 部

辣 là 12.1

170 青部

静 jìng 18b

171 其部

其 qí 13.1

172 雨部

雨 yǔ 10.1
雪 xuě 22.1
零 líng IC1

173 齿部

174 黾部

175 隹部

隹 zhuī Rad
难 nán 7.1

176 金部

金 jīn 14.1

177 鱼部

鱼 yú 12.2
鲜 xiān 19.2

178 革部

鞋 xié 9.2

179 骨部

180 鬼部

181 食部

食 shí Rad
餐 cān 8.1

182 音部

音 yīn 4.1

183 鬥部

184 髟部

185 麻部

麻 má 11.1

186 鹿部

187 黑部

黑 hēi 9.2

188 鼠部

189 鼻部

鼻 bí 15.2